Public
Policy
Skills

Includes Appendix:
The New York Times As An Information Source

by

William D. Coplin

and

Michael K. O'Leary

Professors, Maxwell School of Citizenship
and Public Affairs, Syracuse University

Copyright © 1988 by William D. Coplin and Michael K. O'Leary

All rights reserved

ISBN 0-936826-30-4

Printed in the United States of America

Published by:

Policy Studies Associates
P.O. Box 337
Croton-on-Hudson, NY 10520

Policy Studies Associates (PSA) was established in 1976 to help develop policy analyses skills and apply these to important public issues. An operating program of the Council on International and Public Affairs, PSA is a cooperative non-profit undertaking of a small group of faculty members, teachers, and other educators concerned with improving the quality of education on public policy issues in schools, colleges, and universities.

In 1986, PSA initiated the Effective Participation in Government Program to assist secondary schools, teachers, and students in introducing courses of study which emphasize informal participation in government and community affairs. EPG organizes teacher workshops, provides consultative assistance to schools, and publishes instructional material for teachers and students. For further information write: EPG, Box 632, Fayetteville, New York 13066, or call (315) 637-9650. For all orders, contact: PSA Associates, Box 337, Croton-on-Hudson, NY 10520, or call (914) 271-2039.

ACKNOWLEDGEMENT

Public Policy Skills is a thoroughly revised version of the *Public Policy Study Skills Manual*, published in 1986. Eric Jones, Sarah O'Leary, and Keith Walsh have offered particularly valuable contributions to this book's development, for which we thank them. The many high school teachers associated with Syracuse University's Project Advance have provided excellent critiques and suggestions. Our thanks also go to Midge Longley of *The New York Times* for helping us to create what we feel to be an important addition to this honors text: *The New York Times as an Information Source.*

The many contributions made to the development and refining of our *Effective Participation in Government: A Guide to Policy Skills* and to our *Effective Participation in Government: A Problem-Solving Manual* have helped us in our revisions of this text. In particular, we wish to thank James Carroll for his assistance and the many teachers and students previously acknowledged in those earlier books. Our thanks also go to Marcella Stark and Leslie Pease of Syracuse University's Bird Library for many substantive suggestions in improving Chapter 4.

Maryrose Eannace provided editorial help for the entire manuscript. Mary Pat Daley offered her fine proof-reading skills. Patricia Schuster provided word processing services for our many, many revisions.

ABOUT THE AUTHORS

William D. Coplin is Professor of Public Affairs, and Director of the Public Affairs Program of the Maxwell School at Syracuse University. As contributing author to the guidelines for the Regents twelfth grade required course (1988-89) "Participation in Government," Dr. Coplin was able to draw upon his years of teaching and expertise in public policy analysis and social science education. He has published more than 50 books and articles in the social science and political science fields.

Professor Coplin, who received his Ph.D. from American University, was selected as the Outstanding Undergraduate Teacher for 1986-1987 by the College of Arts and Sciences at Syracuse University. He is a Director of Political Risk Services at Frost and Sullivan, Inc., which provides forecasts of political conditions to more than 1,000 international business clients. He has co-authored Power Persuasion: A Surefire System to Get Ahead in Business (Addison-Wesley, 1985), which was selected by Fortune Book of the Month Club and has been translated into German, Japanese, and Spanish.

Michael K. O'Leary is a professor of political science at the Maxwell School of Citizenship and Public Affairs at Syracuse University. In addition to his research and publications (totaling some 50 books and articles in the fields of international policy analysis, international economic policy, research methods, and teaching strategies), he is contributing author to New York State's guidelines for the "Participation in Government" course. Dr. O'Leary has also served as an editor of the monthly Political Risk Newsletter, and has provided political risk forecasting consultations to multinational firms in this country and abroad.

Dr. O'Leary received his Ph.D. degree from Princeton University. He taught there and at the University of Southern California and Dartmouth College before becoming a faculty member at the Maxwell School in 1965.

TABLE OF CONTENTS

INTRODUCTION

A public policy is a government action that affects what happens in society. Public policy decisions are being made constantly that affect your daily life. Where you go to school, what courses are available for you to study, what jobs will be available to you when you complete your education, when you are allowed to get a driver's license, and how fast you are allowed to drive— all are results of government public policy. To be a part of those decision-making processes in your local, state, national, and international communities, you need to acquire the skills necessary for analyzing and judging actual and proposed policies.

Public Policy Skills will help you learn how to analyze public policy issues in a systematic and well-informed way. It provides you with the conceptual, information-gathering, and analytic skills that are required to make intelligent judgments about existing and proposed public policies.

Each chapter of this book includes hands-on tasks in the steps that create a public policy. All of the chapters, with the exception of Chapter 13, follow the same format. Study that format below for a preview of what to expect:

CHAPTER FORMAT

Opening Section

Each chapter begins with a goal statement that tells you exactly what you will be able to do after successfully completing the work in the chapter. It is followed by an introduction which outlines how the skills presented in the chapter are important for participating in government.

Step Sections

Each chapter contains a series of sections called steps. The step section gives you a specific task such as "identify public policies." The section is divided into two parts:
1. The ideas necessary to complete the step are presented using an example of their application.
2. An exercise with a completed sample is provided. (If your class is using the *Public Policy Skills Workbook*, you will complete exercises in the blank forms provided in the workbook.)

Participation Activities

At the end of Chapters 4, 5, 7, 8, 9, 11, and 12, you will find Participation Activities. These provide concrete opportunities to use your newly acquired skills, while actually contributing to the making of public policies.

APPENDIX A: *The New York Times* As An Information Source

This appendix introduces the *New York Times* as a source of information in the study of public policy issues. The skills taught in this appendix are especially useful in exercises 1.1, 1.2; 3.1–3.6, 7.2–7.7; and in your in-depth study of public policy issues required for Chapters 8 through 12. You will find it useful to review the appendix before you begin studying the text.

APPENDIX B: The Good Society Exercise

This exercise provides an opportunity to explore the principles of justice, order, freedom, and equality. All of the elements necessary for the exercise are included in the Appendix.

1

PART I: BASIC CONCEPTS

This section provides you with the working definitions of several key concepts that you will need to master public policy analysis tasks.

Chapter 1: Components of Public Policy Issues

Step 1: Identifying Public Policies

Step 2: Identifying Public Policy Issues

Chapter 2: Goal Conflicts and Public Policy Issues

Step 1: Identifying Goals in Public Policy Issues

Step 2: Recognizing Private and Public Interests

Step 3: Identifying Goals and Means as a Source of Disagreement

Step 4: Exploring the Role of Private and Public Interest Goals

Chapter 3: Different Types of Public Policy Analysis

Step 1: Monitoring Social Conditions

Step 2: Explaining Social Conditions

Step 3: Forecasting Social Conditions

Step 4: Evaluating Social Conditions

Step 5: Prescribing Public Policy

2

CHAPTER 1

COMPONENTS OF PUBLIC POLICY ISSUES

YOUR GOAL

To identify public policy issues and recognize the social conditions, players, and public policies that are relevant to any given issue.

INTRODUCTION

To become an effective participant in government, you need to be able to identify public policy issues and to recognize their essential features. This chapter introduces you to the basic terms used to identify and classify public policy issues.

A public policy issue develops when an existing or proposed government action has a broad impact on society and is controversial. Radio, television, and newspaper coverage of government and politics frequently focuses on personalities of the politicians. This sometimes makes it difficult to clearly identify the public policy issue. As you work through this section you will find yourself more able to direct your attention to the issues.

3

STEP 1.1
IDENTIFYING PUBLIC POLICIES

What Is a Public Policy?

A public policy is one or more government actions. It is the actual or proposed government action intended to deal with a given social condition. An example of a public policy is requiring all passengers in the front seat of an automobile in New York State to wear a seatbelt.

Since public policy involves government action, we need to recognize the different ways government takes action.

Elements of Public Policies

There are three elements of government actions:

1. Legislation
2. Administrative Acts
3. Judicial Decisions

The **legislation** in a public policy establishes guidelines to be followed by members of the society. A law raising the drinking age from 19 to 21 is intended to stop people between the ages of 19 and 21 from consuming alcoholic beverages. Notice that a law does not necessarily mean that people will behave differently. Governments cannot make people do anything. They can only tell them what is legal behavior and punish them if they act illegally.

Administrative acts are what governments do to put a law into practice. They include such actions as mailing social security checks, giving tickets to people who illegally park their cars, or scheduling when trash will be collected on what streets. Administrative acts are often even more important than the laws themselves. For example, if the police decide not to enforce vigorously the legal drinking age, the law will have little effect on those under 21.

Judicial decisions take place when courts apply the law to a specific situation. They may have the effect of both administrative and legislative acts. For example, existing laws may be declared unconstitutional. The legal situation then returns to the way it was before the law was passed. Also, judges may issue sentences to law violators in ways that either increase or decrease the force of the law. For example, since the early 1980s, violations of drunk driving laws have resulted in harsher penalties in part because judges have gotten tougher.

All three types of government actions are required for any given public policy. For example, to reduce the number of highway accidents, a state sets speed limits on its roads. Making and carrying out such policies involve legislation, administrative acts, and judicial decisions. The legislature of the state enacts general legislation; the Department of Transportation in the state determines the actual limit for a particular stretch of road; and the local courts decide on penalties for people who break the speed limit.

4

Levels of Public Policies

A second general distinction that is made when discussing public policies is the level of government at which the action will take place. The four levels of government actions most often used are:

1. Local—village, town, city or county

2. State—one of the 50 in the United States

3. National—applying to the entire United States

4. International—two or more national governments or international organizations

EXAMPLE

EXERCISE 1.1: IDENTIFYING PUBLIC POLICIES

IN THE TABLE BELOW, PROVIDE EXAMPLES OF EACH OF THE THREE ELEMENTS OF PUBLIC POLICY–LEGISLATION, ADMINISTRATIVE ACTS, OR JUDICIAL DECISIONS–AT EACH OF THE FOUR GOVERNMENT LEVELS:

TYPES OF PUBLIC POLICIES

LEVEL	LEGISLATION	ADMINISTRATIVE ACTS	JUDICIAL DECISIONS
LOCAL	City Council passes legislation establishing a town zoning board	Town zoning board permits construction of a shopping mall building	Judge issues an injunction against building a shopping mall in a zoned area
STATE	Legislature passes and governor signs law requiring drivers to wear seatbelts	State police establish roadblocks to check for violations of the seatbelt law	New York State Court of Appeals upholds state seatbelt law
NATIONAL	Congress passes and President signs law requiring 18-year-old males to register for the draft	Defense Department mails voter registration cards to all 18-year-old males	U.S. Supreme Court upholds the constitutionality of draft registration
INTERN'L	All governments agree by treaty that foreign diplomats are exempt from arrest	Diplomatic pouches are not searched by customs officials	National courts do not have jurisdiction over foreign diplomats in the host country

6

STEP 1.2
IDENTIFYING PUBLIC POLICY ISSUES

What Is a Public Policy Issue?

To determine if a situation is a public policy issue, you would have to answer "yes" to all three of these questions:

1. *Is a public policy involved?*

Public policies are existing or proposed government actions that are the focal point of the issue. This component has been thoroughly described in Step 1.1. Please review it.

2. *Is the policy intended to have an impact on social conditions?*

A **social condition** may include the physical environment, people's behavior, and people's attitudes. Social conditions are usually described by economic and social indicators and can be traced to the public policy in question. For example, the 55-mile speed limit has an effect on a variety of social conditions including the amount of gasoline consumed and the number of automobile accidents. However, physical indicators such as these measure only some of the social conditions affected by the law. The attitudes of people in the society are also a social condition. For example, many people believe they are unfairly restricted by the 55-mile per hour speed limit. This belief may create ill-feeling toward the government and even a willingness to break the law. When identifying social conditions affected by a public policy, include people's attitudes as well as economic and physical indicators.

3. *Do the players disagree over the policy or the social conditions?*

Players are individuals, groups, or institutions that work to shape public policies. Players can be elected officials, appointed officials, organized groups, or private individuals who seek to shape policy.

Unorganized categories of people such as the public, voters, consumers, or taxpayers are not automatically players. To be players, these people have to take an active role in influencing players who are directly involved in a public policy issue. Do not assume people are players merely because they are affected by the public policy. Dog owners are affected by leash laws, but they are not players unless they organize to try to affect policy. To be a player, a person must be actively attempting to influence the public policy process. For example, the players involved in the speed limit policy are legislators, the President, an official of the Department of Transportation, and the state police. A truckers' association that opposes the law, and the American Automobile Association (AAA) which supports the law, also qualify as players.

Components of Public Policy Issues

Public Policy Issue = Public Policy + Social Conditions + Conflicting Players

---

7

Consider the following three situations. Each of them contains one or two elements of our definition of public policy issues, but none contains all of the three required for classification as an issue.

1. Citizens of Columbus, Ohio accept a slight increase in their property taxes.

2. The mayor of Chicago, Illinois runs for re-election.

3. A sparse rainfall in parts of two Southern states creates hardship for many farmers.

(1) Raising property taxes in Columbus, Ohio constitutes a public policy dealing with a social condition. But without any disagreement over the decision, it does not become a public policy issue. (2) A mayor's re-election campaign may involve disagreement among important groups within the city's voting public regarding the governmental actions that will follow as a consequence of the election results. However, the election itself does not represent a *social condition*. (3) The low rainfall statement indicates a social condition and some desire for action on the part of those farmers affected, but no widespread call for action; in such case, the likelihood of a government action is low.

Any of the three incidents could evolve into a public policy issue. To illustrate, we have changed the examples so that they satisfy the three requirements for being considered as public policy issues.

1. Many citizens of Columbus oppose an attempted increase in property taxes.

2. The mayor has declared that his re-election will signify support for a policy of extensive urban renewal in all decaying urban areas. His opponents oppose him primarily on this declaration.

3. A substantial increase in federal or state governmental aid is requested to assist the farmers affected by drought, but some people feel the government cannot afford to increase the aid levels.

8

EXAMPLE

EXERCISE 1.2: IDENTIFYING PUBLIC POLICY ISSUES

IDENTIFY THREE PUBLIC POLICY ISSUES AND BRIEFLY DESCRIBE HOW EACH MEETS THE ESSENTIAL REQUIREMENTS: 1) DISAGREEMENT AMONG PLAYERS, 2) SOCIAL CONDITIONS, 3) PUBLIC POLICY:

ISSUE 1: Should New York State have a 21-year-old drinking age law?

REQUIREMENTS:

This issue meets the three requirements outlined above. It consists of a potential policy (a proposed piece of legislation to require an individual to be at least 21 years old to consume alcohol beverages), a disagreement among identifiable groups in the society (representatives of the liquor industry and groups like Students Against Drunk Driving (SADD) concerned with alcohol-related accidents), and social conditions (number of traffic fatalities related to alcohol).

ISSUE 2: Should the United States government negotiate with terrorists for the release of hostages?

REQUIREMENTS:

This issue meets the three requirements outlined above. It consists of: a disagreement between those who say negotiating encourages future terrorist activities and those members of the hostages' families and supporters of human rights who say that it is more important to save lives; social conditions such as the safety of people traveling in the affected region and media coverage of the terrorists' cause; and a possible decision to meet with representatives of the terrorists.

ISSUE 3: Should public schools allow time for prayer?

REQUIREMENTS:

The issue involves disagreement (students and parents who feel their constitutional rights are being violated and school officials that do allow time for prayer), social conditions (the attitude of citizens who fear the country is becoming religious in nature—or the opposite, Godless), and public policy (a possible court order to prohibit or permit prayer).

SUMMARY

CONCEPTS	DEFINITIONS	SKILLS	EXAMPLES
Social Conditions	The conditions in society that have generated the issue	Identify what conditions in the society have generated the issue	Inflation Unemployment Crime rate Attitudes toward police
Public Policies	The actual or proposed government actions intended to deal with the social conditions	Describe public policies or government actions that are aimed at dealing with social conditions	Price controls Job corp program Increased police budget Student loan program School busing
Players	The individuals, organized groups,or institutions that consciously work to shape public policy	List players that consciously seek to shape public policy. Include players on all sides of an issue	Ralph Nader Mayor League of Women Voters Heritage Foundation Secretary of Defense
Public Policy Issue	Public Policy Issue = Public Policy + Social Conditions + Conflicting Players	Identify a public policy issue	Should the federal government provide aid to assist farmers affected by drought?

10

CHAPTER 2

GOAL CONFLICTS AND PUBLIC POLICY ISSUES

YOUR GOAL

To identify goals that motivate players on public policy issues and to distinguish between private and public interest goals.

INTRODUCTION

Did you ever wonder why some people get so upset about public policy issues and why many issues never seem to be resolved? The reason is that players are motivated by different goals, that is, different ideas of what are desirable social conditions. These motivations are frequently very strong, and they may set in motion intense conflict.

At a personal level, it is easy to see why different goals can lead to conflict. Whether you or your brother (if you have one) gets the car Saturday night can lead to tension. At a different level, players can engage in conflict over public policy issues. Lower taxes for one group might mean higher taxes for another. Prayer in school would represent a gain for those who support it, but a loss for its opponents. The seatbelt law is supported by those who see the cost of insurance being reduced and opposed by those who see their freedom decreased. Although the "fight" is not usually in physical terms, it is nonetheless just as intense. In extreme cases, it can result in violence. For example, protests over America's Vietnam policies in the 1960s and early 1970s sometimes led to violence. Today, some extreme anti-abortion groups have bombed clinics that provide information on abortion and birth control.

Goal conflicts over public policy issues are more complex than the goal conflicts over personal issues. Most public policy issues involve many players, each with slightly different goals. On income tax reform, for example, some provisions might benefit the rich, others the middle class, and still others the poor. Conflict arises in part because the rich and some of the middle class believe that the system must help to stimulate business, and therefore should take less income of business and wealthy people.

STEP 2.1
IDENTIFYING GOALS IN PUBLIC POLICY ISSUES

It is important for the analyst of public policy issues to be clear about the goals of players. When applied to public policy issues, goals are defined as social conditions preferred by one or more players. Whether acting as individuals or groups, players seek public policies that:

- Promote social conditions they consider desirable

- Eliminate or minimize social conditions they consider undesirable

For example, farm groups seek public policies that increase the income they receive from their products. The Audubon Society seeks to make the environment safer for birds. The Public Health Service seeks to reduce the risks from disease.

It is useful to examine the motivations of a variety of players when exploring the goals creating a public policy issue. One initial approach is to look at a specific public policy proposal and identify a goal that motivates supporters of the policy and a goal that motivates the opposition. You can determine these goals by examining what the players say. What you know about their self-interests and views of the world can also help you to understand their goals.

EXAMPLE

EXERCISE 2.1: IDENTIFYING GOALS IN PUBLIC POLICY ISSUES

IDENTIFY A PUBLIC POLICY:

The public policy is to increase federal government spending on nuclear weapons.

IDENTIFY ONE GOAL OF PLAYERS THAT SUPPORT THE POLICY:

The proponents of more spending believe that this will reduce the threat of nuclear war.

IDENTIFY ONE GOAL OF PLAYERS THAT OPPOSE THE POLICY:

The opponents of more spending believe that the government deficit must be reduced.

STEP 2.2
RECOGNIZING PRIVATE AND PUBLIC INTERESTS

The goals pursued by players can be justified on two different grounds–private interests and public interests. It is important to distinguish between the two.

Under the justification of private interest, the player pursues a goal because it will benefit the player directly. Private interests often involve money in one way or another. Corporations want lower taxes, farmers want subsidies for their products, police officers want higher salaries. Some private interests represent non-economic goals. For example, homeowners want the best street maintenance on their own block. If you have a question as to whether a goal is a private interest, ask yourself the question: "Is the benefit received directly and exclusively by the player?"

Players pursue public interest goals because they feel the society as a whole will benefit. Examples of public interest goals include preserving the national security and building an interstate highway. In both cases, everyone in the society benefits or can benefit from the achievement of the goal. Remember that the society to which the public interest refers is related to the level of government–local, state, national, or international.

Some of the most powerful public interests are stated in general terms. They include the following:

- Individual freedom—the right of individuals to think, speak and act as they wish as long as it does not infringe on the freedom of others

- National security—the ability of a country to defend itself against the domination or physical destruction by a foreign army

- Social order—the maintenance of peace and the consistent operation of laws within a society

- Equality—the idea that each member of a community is equal to other members of the community

- Justice—the fair treatment of individuals by the government and by others in society

The existence of these public interests is evident in the Declaration of Independence. Figure 2.1 on the following page lists passages representing each of the five public interests discussed.

14

Figure 2.1: Public Interests Evident in the Declaration of Independence

INTANGIBLE PUBLIC INTERESTS	QUOTATION FROM DECLARATION OF INDEPENDENCE
• Individual Freedom	"Life, Liberty and the pursuit of Happiness"
• National Security	"He is at this time transporting large armies of foreign mercenaries to complete the works of death, desolation and tyranny"
• Social Order	"He has excited domestic insurrections amongst us..."
• Equality	"All men are created equal"
• Justice	"For depriving us in many cases of the benefits of Trial by Jury"

Other less general public interest goals are:

- Physical survival for members of the society

- Full employment

- Good education

- Safe roads

- High standard of living

- Clean air and water

- Less crime

These public interest goals frequently affect public policy decisions.

Any goal pursued by any player can be justified on grounds of both public and private interests. Even though the Declaration of Independence made the argument for independence primarily on the grounds of public interests, it is clear that private interests were at work. The phrase "pursuit of happiness" is a statement that was important to many private individuals and groups. They felt they could not derive the personal benefits they wanted under British rule. From studies of the period, we also know that British policies restricting what could be manufactured and exported were an important motivation to businessmen in the Colonies.

In general, public interest justifications are made more frequently and more openly than private interest justifications. The reason for this is simple. A player seeking to gain support for a policy can broaden its appeal by claiming the public interest is served. The public interest is sometimes used as a cover-up for private interests. However, governments and people do take actions for the good of the society as a whole, and this sometimes helps some private interests and harms others.

EXAMPLE

EXERCISE 2.2: RECOGNIZING PRIVATE AND PUBLIC INTERESTS

IDENTIFY A PUBLIC POLICY:

Establish the 21-Year-Old Drinking Age Law in New York State

IDENTIFY A PUBLIC INTEREST THAT UNDERLIES THE POSITIONS OF:

SUPPORTING PLAYERS

Social order: alcohol
consumption increases
the chance of lawless
behavior.

OPPOSING PLAYERS

Justice: if
18-year-olds are
asked to fight
for their country,
they should be able
to consume alcohol.

IDENTIFY A PRIVATE INTEREST THAT UNDERLIES THE POSITION OF:

SUPPORTING PLAYERS

Parents' desire to control
their children's drinking:
law will help parents in
their fight to keep their
teenagers from consuming
alcohol.

OPPOSING PLAYERS

Profit: if drinking
age is raised,
revenues to bar owners
will be reduced.

STEP 2.3
IDENTIFYING GOALS AND MEANS
AS A SOURCE OF DISAGREEMENT

Public policy issues arise because there are disagreements among players. Aside from poor personal relationships or poor communications among the players, there are two sources of disagreements:

1. *Goals*—Players who support a given policy may have different goals or attach a higher priority to different goals than players who oppose the policy.

> ### Example of Differences Over Goals
>
> The goal of supporters of capital punishment is to deter crimes; the goal of opponents is to avoid a public policy that takes human life.

2. *Means*—Players may agree on goals for the most part but either do not think the policy is the best way to achieve the goals or think that the policy would create more serious problems than the problem it would correct.

> ### Example of Differences Over Means
>
> Some people support government spending to reduce unemployment; others oppose government spending because they feel it leads to inflation and other consequences that, in the long run, increase unemployment.

Differences over goals, or at least the relative priority attached to them is a major source of conflict for many public policy issues. In this case, players supporting a policy do not share the same goal or give it the same level of importance as players opposing the policy. For example, those supporting a mandatory seatbelt law place a higher value on the preservation of human life than those opposing the seatbelt law. The latter appears to consider freedom of choice to be a high value. In some cases the disagreement may not be as obvious because both sides say they share the same goal but, in fact, *disagree as to the interpretation of the same goal.* Players on both sides may claim that they support the same general goal but disagree over how that goal would be defined or applied with respect to a specific policy. For example, both sides on the mandatory seatbelt issue might say their positions are a matter of justice. Those supporting the law might argue that it is unjust to pay higher insurance rates because people will not voluntarily wear seatbelts, while those opposing the law might argue that it is unjust for the government to enforce the majority's opinion on the minority that might choose not to wear seatbelts.

Disagreement on the policy to achieve the goal, that is, difference over means, is also a source of conflict in public policy issues. In this case, both sides share the same specific goals and define it in the same way. The goal itself is not the source of disagreement over the policy; instead, the disagreement is over the best way to achieve the policy. In the seatbelt example, both sides might agree that reducing deaths and injuries from highway accidents is the desirable goal. Those supporting mandatory seatbelt legislation would argue that this policy would have a major impact on reducing injury and deaths. Those opposing the legislation might argue that putting the same government resources in driver education programs would lead to a larger reduction in injuries and deaths.

Players can disagree over means also because one player feels that a particular policy has more serious negative consequences than the problem it was initially designed to attack. Many of those opposing the mandatory seatbelt law feel that the loss of freedom is so wrong that the law should be repealed regardless of the number of lives it saves.

When analyzing the reasons players have for supporting or opposing a specific policy, you need to decide what the points of disagreement are. You can do this by listing the major goals of both sides and their attitudes toward the existing policy and proposals for other policies. One difficulty in completing such an analysis is that varieties of considerations usually motivate players' behavior. Another is that players usually use general public interest goals in their discussions, but are really motivated by more narrow private interest goals. For example, on the mandatory seatbelt law, those against the law on the grounds of preserving individual freedom may be motivated just as much by their own personal desire not to wear seatbelts, and those for the law on grounds of reducing traffic deaths may be motivated just as much by the desire for lower insurance rates.

EXAMPLE

EXERCISE 2.3: IDENTIFYING GOALS AND MEANS
AS A SOURCE OF DISAGREEMENT

(A) IDENTIFY A PUBLIC POLICY ISSUE (YOU MAY USE THE POLICY YOU USED IN EXERCISE 2.2, IF YOU WISH.):

Establishing a 21 year-old minimum drinking age.

(B) IDENTIFY A MAJOR DIFFERENCE OVER GOALS BETWEEN PLAYERS. IDENTIFY AT LEAST ONE GOAL ON EACH SIDE:

The major difference between those who support and those who oppose the law is that the former value the preservation of human life as the most important public interest, while the latter value individual freedom (for those between 19 and 21) as the most important public interest.

(C) IDENTIFY A GOAL WHICH BOTH PLAYERS SHARE AND DEFINE IN THE SAME WAY. INDICATE WHAT POLICY THE OPPOSING PLAYER WOULD SUPPORT RATHER THAN THE ONE STATED ABOVE:

Both players would like to see fewer traffic fatalities from drunk driving. Opponents to the 21 year-old drinking age would argue that harsher penalties against drunk driving would be a more effective way to achieve that goal.

STEP 2.4
EXPLORING THE ROLE OF PRIVATE
AND PUBLIC INTEREST GOALS

One type of policy by which you as a student are greatly affected is the grading policy operating in your class. How your teacher assigns grades has a significant impact on your life. The following exercise enables you to have direct experience in the making of a policy that affects you and helps you explore the role public and private interest goals play in shaping your behavior and the behavior of your class. The exercise gives you the opportunity to select how letter grades will be assigned to the numerical score you achieve on assignments and tests for this class. (Your teacher may choose to run this exercise as a simulation in which the results are not binding.)

OVERVIEW

This exercise assumes that your teacher now marks according to a traditional system in which letter grades are allocated in the following way:

Grade	Numerical Score
A	90 - 100
B	80 - 89
C	70 - 79
D	60 - 69
F	Below 60

After a period of class discussion, you will reach a decision as to which of the following three grading systems your class will use:

1. *Traditional* system as described above.

2. *Conservative* system in which students who receive the top 35% of the scores receive an A; the next 15% receive a B; the next 35% receive a C; the next 10% receive a D; and the remaining 5% receive an F.

3. *Socialist* system in which the students who receive the top 10% receive an A; the next 60% receive a B; the next 15% receive a C; the next 10% receive a D; and the remaining 5% receive an F.

   NOTE: If either the Conservative or Socialist system is chosen, students who would be better off with the Traditional system will receive the grade designated under the Traditional system. The Conservative and Socialist systems are subsidies to benefit different types of students. They cannot be used to penalize students who would be better off under the traditional system.

By participating in the exercise, you will learn about the conflict among groups with different interests, the relationship of self-interest and such public interest values as freedom, order, equality, justice, minority and majority rights, and the legitimacy of decision-making processes.

21

PROCEDURES

The exercise should take two class periods. During the *first* period, you will discuss the pro's and con's of the three options. A procedure for this discussion called *The Somoan Circle* will be used. It works in the following way:

1. Five chairs will be placed in a circle at the front of the room.

2. You may speak only if you sit in one of the five chairs.

3. If you are in your regular seat, you may not speak.

4. Come up and sit in one of the chairs when you are ready to speak. You can remain in the chair if you think you might want to say something more. If, however, another classmate from the audience stands behind you, you must return to your regular seat until another seat is open.

5. You may say anything you want while you are in one of the five chairs and as long as you respect the other members of the class sitting in the other chairs. Remember to state your views clearly and briefly. Don't ramble.

During the *second* period, your class will make a decision according to the following rules:

1. The final policy must be either the Traditional, Conservative, or Socialist system.

2. If you fail to reach a decision by the end of the exercise, the Traditional system will stay in effect.

3. Your instructor will chair the class meeting.

4. The class can reach a decision in one of two ways:
   a. By unanimous agreement of everyone in the class on one of the three options.

   b. If no unanimous agreement can be reached on one of the three options, the class can decide on a voting procedure such as two-thirds majority, simple majority, or any other procedure. However, there must be unanimous agreement on the voting procedure.

5. Unruly behavior will result in the instructor requiring one minute of silence.

DEBRIEFING

Once you have participated in the grading exercise, you should be able to explore the kinds of goals that motivated you, your classmates, and your instructor.

Public goals that may have motivated some include the following:

1. Maintaining order
2. Promoting equality

22

3. Creating a more just system

4. Promoting more learning

5. Protecting majority rights

6. Protecting minority rights

Private interest goals that may have motivated some could include the following:

1. Less stress

2. Less work

3. Higher grades

The kinds of goals and questions raised by the grading exercise can be found in almost every public policy issue. All public policies benefit some segments of the society and harm some segments, just as the traditionalist system would result in lower grades for the less hardworking members of the class than would the socialist system. The conflict between majority and minority rights which always develops in the exercise is similar to the conflict between the majority and minority over voting rights and equality of opportunity in the United States. To the extent that the conservative and socialist systems are systems that provide subsidies to different groups, they raise questions similar to those raised about subsidies to farmers, tax credits to business, and tariffs on imports.

Disagreement among players in the grading exercise can also occur over means. Both sides may accept increased learning as a major goal; but those calling for a socialist system might argue that by reducing the stress over grades more learning would be achieved, while those calling for the traditionalist system would say that competition produces more learning.

You should also recognize in your behavior and the behavior of others the relative strength of public and private interests. You may be looking for a higher grade for yourself, but are putting your arguments in more public interest terms (e.g., the class would learn more). Even traditionalists, who have argued that they are only trying to preserve order, have been accused of trying to get more personal satisfaction by raising the level of competition in the class.

A variety of analogies can be developed relating what has happened in the grading exercise to past and current real world public policy issues. Look for the similarities and realize that public policies at the local, state, and federal levels will have a direct impact on goals that you find important to yourself personally and to the society in which you live.

EXAMPLE

EXERCISE 2.4: EXPLORING THE ROLE OF PRIVATE AND PUBLIC INTEREST GOALS

USING A PAST OR CURRENT PUBLIC POLICY ISSUE, COMPARE HOW THE GRADING EXERCISE IS SIMILAR TO THE ISSUE YOU HAVE CHOSEN:

In the grading exercise, several traditionalists made arguments similar to those who argue against tariffs in the United States. Traditionalists said that maintaining high standards and not creating any artificial benefits, would produce students who learn more. The idea behind this argument is similar to the idea behind those arguing for free trade. It is assumed that competing for grades against an absolute standard is similar to competing for sales against the best standards available from any place in the world. The major public interest goal behind the traditionalist viewpoint is to maximize learning. The major public interest goal behind those opposed to tariffs is to maximize productivity.

SUMMARY

CONCEPTS	DEFINITIONS	SKILLS	EXAMPLES
Goal	Preferred social condition motivating players	Identify goals	Less loss of life through traffic accidents
Private Interest	Goal pursued for direct benefit to the player	List private interests of players	Landowner receiving a building permit
Public Interest	Goal assumed to benefit the whole society	List a public interest	Building a new highway
Means	Policy pursued to achieve a goal	Identify means	Implement a mandatory seatbelt law

CHAPTER 3

DIFFERENT TYPES OF PUBLIC POLICY ANALYSIS

YOUR GOAL

To identify and assess the five types of public policy analysis.

INTRODUCTION

A good analyst uses the following five types of analysis when discussing a public policy issue.

1. Monitoring social conditions
2. Explaining social conditions
3. Forecasting social conditions
4. Evaluating social conditions
5. Prescribing public policy

This chapter will help you to identify which types of public policy analysis are presented in a speech, book, or article. The exercises in this chapter give you practice in identifying and assessing the five types of public policy analysis.

Read the article on the next page before looking at the examples that follow.

Mental Health on the Street

It remains to be seen whether Joyce Brown's release from the hospital to a residential program puts a happy ending to the story of a homeless woman's fight against involuntary psychiatric treatment. Beyond law, her case dramatizes the failure of a policy — deinstitutionalization, the emptying of state mental hospitals during the 1970's.

Now New York proposes to become the first state to start rectifying that failure on a statewide basis. Richard Surles, Governor Cuomo's new choice as commissioner of mental health, proposes to alter mental health care delivery in a bold way that would make it harder for the system to lose the Joyce Browns. The experiment deserves local approval and national attention.

The mental health planners who promoted deinstitutionalization in New York and elsewhere could never have imagined creating a generation of homeless Joyce Browns. Community programs were supposed to provide adequate shelter and treatment once patients were discharged from big state mental hospitals. But the community care never materialized.

One reason was political: Towns and unions dependent on the big institutions limited the transfer of funds to cities where most of the mentally ill went to live. In recent years, the Cuomo administration has chipped away at this outrage, winning approval for more spending in communities. Dr. Surles would provide yet more — but with a crucial difference. Money for community mental health now goes to established programs and agencies. While many offer wonderful services, they require that patients come to them. The most desperate patients — wandering the streets, showing up occasionally at city shelters, bouncing in and out of hospital wards — aren't likely to enroll.

Dr. Surles would therefore create a corps of "case managers" to seek them out. Each mental health worker would be assigned no more than 10 patients, and would follow them on the streets if necessary. Case managers would try persuading their clients to come in for treatment, make sure they take their medication, provide continuing support.

The proposal recognizes that community health care depends as much on the availability of services as on such outreach. Each case manager therefore could draw upon $4,000 per year in state funds for each client. That would permit expansion of programs tailored to actual needs. In theory at least, fewer Joyce Browns could fall through the cracks.

Dr. Surles would begin with 500 case managers dealing with 5,000 patients statewide at a cost of $35 million annually — money linked to patients rather than institutions. It's a creative and humane idea and a sensible investment.

New York Times, January 29, 1988. Copyright © 1988. Reprinted by permission.

STEP 3.1
MONITORING SOCIAL CONDITIONS

Monitoring social conditions is the process of observing and recording what is happening in society that gives rise to public policy issues. Like the biologist who carefully observes nature, the public policy analyst collects information about society. In the box below are some typical examples of monitoring.

Examples of Monitoring Social Conditions

The federal debt increased from less that $1 trillion in 1980 to $2.2 trillion in 1987.

The New York State Office of Advocate for the Disabled information telephone referral service answered 11,988 calls in 1986, up 6% from 1985.

In 1980, there were an estimated 2.2 million homeless persons.

Guidelines for Monitoring

1. **Present clear and precise information.** Look for a clear and specific description of social conditions.

Bad Example:	Traffic fatalities in New York State are very high.	Good Example:	Traffic fatalities in New York State for the years 1980-1984 were 7% above the national average.

29

2. **Give information that is as complete as possible.** Testing for completeness can be done in three ways:

   A. Does the information provided allow for a comparison of conditions over time? It is better to know the number of traffic fatalities for each of the past five years than for only the most recent year.

   B. Does the information make an effort to cover all parts of the society or does it deal with only certain areas or groups? In a study of New York State, reports on traffic fatalities in just New York City would not be enough.

   C. Does the information provide a basis for comparison?

Bad Example:	In 1981, there were 3.2 traffic fatalities in New York State per 100,000,000 vehicle miles.	Good Example:	In 1981, there were 3.2 traffic fatalities in New York State per 100,000,000 vehicle miles and 5.2 traffic fatalities per 100,000,000 vehicle miles in Wyoming.

3. **Provide evidence that the information is accurate.** Cite books, articles, documents, or surveys used. Numbers and information provided without documentation cannot be trusted as much as those with documentation. Accuracy is always a problem in measuring social conditions, and the more known about how that information was collected the better. For example, the source for the figures cited in the examples above is the 1982 edition of Accident Facts published by the National Safety Council.

EXAMPLE

EXERCISE 3.1: MONITORING SOCIAL CONDITIONS

(A) SELECT AN EDITORIAL OR SIMILAR OPINION PIECE THAT DISCUSSES A PUBLIC POLICY ISSUE. PROVIDE THE SOURCE OF THE ARTICLE:

SOURCE: "Mental Health on the Street", The New York Times, January 25, 1988, page A20.

(B) IDENTIFY AN EXAMPLE OF MONITORING SOCIAL CONDITIONS EXPRESSED IN THE EDITORIAL EITHER BY QUOTING DIRECTLY FROM THE EDITORIAL OR PARAPHRASING WHAT WAS SAID OR IMPLIED:

Most patients do not enroll in existing support programs.

(C) CRITIQUE THE MONITORING OF SOCIAL CONDITIONS. INDICATE BOTH THE STRENGTHS AND WEAKNESSES OF THE ARTICLE BY FOLLOWING THE THREE GUIDELINES POSED IN THE PRECEDING PAGES. NUMBER THE ANSWERS THAT REFER TO EACH GUIDELINE. EITHER GIVE SPECIFIC ILLUSTRATIONS FROM THE EDITORIAL OR SUGGEST HOW THE WRITER MIGHT HAVE SATISFIED THE GUIDELINES PROVIDED:

1. The monitoring information is unclear and imprecise. The author uses the term "desperate patients" with no further definition. No statistics or estimate on how many homeless there are and, of those homeless, how many are seriously mentally ill. The only specific piece of concrete evidence is the reference to the experiences of Joyce Brown.

2. No time perspective is given. Has the number of homeless persons who are mentally ill increased over the past five years? Comparisons with other cities are not presented, and it is not clear how much of the New York metropolitan area is included.

3. No government or academic studies are cited by the author.

31

STEP 3.2
EXPLAINING SOCIAL CONDITIONS

Explaining social conditions is describing what factors contribute to the conditions in society monitored in Step 3.1. If you have ever missed a curfew set by your parents, you may have attempted to explain why you were late. Explanation as a form of public policy analysis is similar, since it requires you to give the reasons why society is the way it is. The box below provides several explanations of different social conditions.

Examples of Explaining Social Conditions

The Congress and administration are not willing to suffer the political consequences of cutting spending or raising taxes.

As disabled advocacy groups gain publicity, more people want to find out how to utilize their services.

Cuts in funding for food stamps, welfare benefits, and housing subsidies have made housing unaffordable for the poor.

Explaining why a condition exists is quite difficult because most social conditions are caused by a large number of factors. For instance, the number of traffic fatalities in California can be affected by the weather, the driving speed, and even the health of the economy. Research can give a general indication of which factors are important, but even the most elaborate studies fail to give absolutely complete explanations.

Guidelines for Good Explaining

1. *Cite as many relevant factors as possible.* Most social conditions are caused by a large number of interacting factors. For example, juvenile delinquency may be caused by broken homes, peer pressure, low self-esteem, and several other factors. Therefore, single-factor explanations are almost always inaccurate. An attempt to consider a large number of factors is a sign that the analyst is trying to be as careful as possible in developing explanations. The following categories of factors should be considered: (1) economic, (2) geographic, (3) sociological, (4) political, and (5) psychological.

2. *Cite academic or government sources to support the factors you list.* For almost every public policy issue, studies exist that identify the causes of the social conditions that have generated the issue. These studies are undertaken by scholars working in universities, research organizations, and also by government agencies. For example, in 1986, *The Final Report of the Attorney General's Commission on Pornography* contended that pornography is one of the factors responsible for a growing number of rapes and acts of violence against women. Chapter 4 will tell you how to locate these studies in the library. A good explanation will cite studies that demonstrate which factors contribute most to a social condition.

EXAMPLE

EXERCISE 3.2: EXPLAINING SOCIAL CONDITIONS

(A) IDENTIFY AN EXAMPLE OF EXPLANATIONS OF SOCIAL CONDITIONS EXPRESSED IN THE EDITORIAL EITHER BY QUOTING DIRECTLY FROM THE EDITORIAL OR PARAPHRASING WHAT WAS SAID OR IMPLIED:

Deinstitutionalization policies in the 1970s caused the number of mentally ill, homeless persons to increase.

(B) CRITIQUE THE EXPLANATION OF SOCIAL CONDITIONS. INDICATE BOTH THE STRENGTHS AND WEAKNESSES OF THE ARTICLE BY FOLLOWING THE TWO GUIDELINES POSED IN THE PRECEDING PAGES. NUMBER THE ANSWERS THAT REFER TO EACH GUIDELINE. EITHER GIVE SPECIFIC ILLUSTRATIONS FROM THE EDITORIAL OR SUGGEST HOW THE WRITER MIGHT HAVE SATISFIED THE GUIDELINES PROVIDED:

1. The author identifies political factors that explain the condition. He should have included economic factors, such as budget cuts, and social factors, such as changing attitudes about deinstitutionalization, in the explanation.

2. No sources are cited to support the role of deinstitutionalization in the growth of the homeless problem. Since many people have argued the importance of this factor, it would have been easy to cite statements by government officials and academic researchers.

STEP 3.3
FORECASTING SOCIAL CONDITIONS

Forecasting social conditions is predicting what social conditions will be like in the future. Like the weather forecaster who attempts to tell you in the middle of the week what the weekend weather will be, the public policy analyst makes forecasts about what society will look like one year, or even ten years, down the road. Unfortunately, like the weather forecaster, uncertainty surrounds forecasts of social conditions. The farther into the future the prediction, the greater the uncertainty. The box below provides forecasts of several different social conditions.

Examples of Forecasting Social Conditions

The American federal debt will double within the next five years.

The number of calls to the Office of Advocate for the Disabled will increase as more people find out about the referral service.

The number of homeless people will increase by 10% annually over the next three years.

Discussions of public policy issues are concerned with the future. All public policies are undertaken either to change future social conditions or to prevent changes. Forecasting, therefore, is critical to any public policy analysis.

Guidelines for Good Forecasting

1. *Be clear with respect to what is being forecast and the time frame of the forecast.* The first statement below is unclear about the amount of increase, the time frame, and even where the rise will occur.

Bad Example:	Traffic fatalities will continue to rise.	Good Example:	For each of the next five years, traffic fatalities in New York State will rise 5% per year.

34

2. *Cite academic or government authorities if possible.* The best forecasts are those that are backed up by government or academic studies and are made by individuals and groups who have expertise and have no vested interest in the conclusion of the forecast. A particularly useful approach is to find a number of forecasts by experts on the issue and to consider all of their viewpoints.

3. *Make reasoning behind the forecast clear.* If you are unable to find academic or government authorities to support your forecast, you will need to make clear your own reasoning for your forecast. Basically, you will make one of two types of forecast:

   A. Things will *continue* as they have in the past. For example, "For each of the next five years, traffic fatalities in New York State will rise 5% per year" could be based on trends over the past decade which show a 5% a year increase.

   B. Things will be *different* from what they have been in the past. For example, the number of traffic deaths will decline by 5% a year over the next five years due to increased use of seatbelts.

Both forecasts are based on the same historical information over the past ten years. However, forecast B assumes that increased use of seatbelts will cause a change in the historical trend. Forecast A, though, assumes that increased seatbelt use will not make a major difference.

EXAMPLE

EXERCISE 3.3: FORECASTING SOCIAL CONDITIONS

(A) IDENTIFY AN EXAMPLE OF FORECASTING SOCIAL CONDITIONS EXPRESSED IN THE EDITORIAL EITHER BY QUOTING DIRECTLY FROM THE EDITORIAL OR PARAPHRASING WHAT WAS SAID OR IMPLIED:

The number of mentally ill persons who become homeless is likely to increase unless new policies are implemented.

(B) CRITIQUE THE FORECASTING OF SOCIAL CONDITIONS. INDICATE BOTH THE STRENGTHS AND WEAKNESSES OF THE ARTICLE BY FOLLOWING THE THREE GUIDELINES POSED IN THE PRECEDING PAGES. NUMBER THE ANSWERS THAT REFER TO EACH GUIDELINE. EITHER GIVE SPECIFIC ILLUSTRATIONS FROM THE EDITORIAL OR SUGGEST HOW THE WRITER MIGHT HAVE SATISFIED THE GUIDELINES PROVIDED:

1. The author merely implies that the increase is likely to continue. He fails to state that assumption clearly and therefore provides no timeframe. He also fails to indicate how much the number of homeless persons will increase.

2. No clear forecast was presented, and no effort was made to document the forecast with government or academic sources.

3. There is no clear rationale for the assumption that the number of homeless persons who are mentally ill will continue to increase. One assumption that might have been stated is that since mental illness continues to be a serious problem in our society and may in fact be increasing, the number of homeless persons is also expected to increase.

STEP 3.4
EVALUATING SOCIAL CONDITIONS

Evaluating social conditions is judging whether conditions in society are desirable or undesirable. A public policy analyst might conclude that the number of traffic fatalities is too high or, if the trend is downward, that conditions are improving. Like teachers who grade your performance, public policy analysts determine whether society is performing up to levels they consider adequate.

Evaluation of social conditions is necessary because the conclusion reached about whether there is too much crime, drug abuse, unemployment, or any other undesirable social condition, leads to decisions about whether new public policies are needed. The box below provides several examples of evaluations of social conditions.

Examples of Evaluating Social Conditions

The federal debt will unfairly burden future generations with staggering bills.

People who call the referral service benefit from being directed to the resource office that can best help them.

Too many homeless persons die from exposure and lack of proper medical care.

Guidelines for Good Evaluating

1. *Be clear in identifying goals that should be used to judge social conditions.* Good public policy analysis requires a clear statement of what social conditions are desired. For example, those supporting the mandatory seatbelt law in New York State have the goal of fewer traffic fatalities. In many cases, the analyst takes for granted that the reader understands the importance of the goal of the analysis.

2. *Consider all major goals that are relevant to the public policy issue.* Most policy issues involve many goals, some consistent with one another, some in conflict. For example, a discussion of the mandatory seatbelt law can begin with the goal of preserving human life, but should identify other goals which may or may not be in conflict with saving lives. Some of these are (1) individual freedom, which many feel is reduced by the law; (2) the respect of government itself because of the difficulty in enforcing the law; (3) increased costs to the taxpayers resulting from the enforcement costs; and (4) reduced car insurance premiums.

37

EXAMPLE

EXERCISE 3.4: EVALUATING SOCIAL CONDITIONS

(A) IDENTIFY AN EXAMPLE OF EVALUATING SOCIAL CONDITIONS EXPRESSED IN THE EDITORIAL EITHER BY QUOTING DIRECTLY FROM THE EDITORIAL OR PARAPHRASING WHAT WAS SAID OR IMPLIED:

The emptying of state mental hospitals has been a failure because it has greatly increased the number of homeless persons.

(B) CRITIQUE THE EVALUATING OF SOCIAL CONDITIONS. INDICATE BOTH THE STRENGTHS AND WEAKNESSES OF THE ARTICLE BY FOLLOWING THE TWO GUIDELINES POSED IN THE PRECEDING PAGES. NUMBER THE ANSWERS THAT REFER TO EACH GUIDELINE. EITHER GIVE SPECIFIC ILLUSTRATIONS FROM THE EDITORIAL OR SUGGEST HOW THE WRITER MIGHT HAVE SATISFIED THE GUIDELINES PROVIDED:

1. Although the writer does not make it clear, we can assume that the number one goal is the desire to reduce the number of homeless persons and a second goal is better treatment of mentally ill persons. The author also mentions the cost of the proposed policy and implies that he would like to have a cost-effective solution.

2. Other goals that might have been mentioned include reducing the number of homeless people who are not suffering from mental illness and reducing some of the factors contributing to mental illness in the first place.

STEP 3.5
PRESCRIBING PUBLIC POLICY

Prescribing public policy is suggesting what government action should be taken to promote good social conditions. For example, the analyst might prescribe a mandatory seatbelt law, as the New York State government did in 1984, to reduce traffic fatalities. Like a medical doctor who prescribes an antibiotic to clear up an infection, the public policy analyst prescribes a government action to reduce undesirable social conditions or promote desirable ones. The box below provides several explanations of different social conditions.

Examples of Prescribing Public Policies

The federal government should double the gasoline tax.

The Office of Advocate for the Disabled should launch a publicity campaign to inform the public of the services they provide.

The amount of federal funds allocated to low-income housing programs should be increased by 50%.

Guidelines for Good Prescribing

1. *Provide a clear prescription.* The analyst must be very clear about which policy is being recommended and at what level of government. Also, a goal should not be confused with a prescription.

Bad Example:	Every car should have an air bag.	Good Example:	The federal government should require all new cars sold in the U.S. to have air bags.

The bad example states a goal rather than a policy and fails to identify a specific level of government.

39

2. *Provide several alternatives to the favored prescription.* While the analysis may strongly endorse a specific policy, it should examine the alternatives. This will demonstrate that the analysis includes all the relevant factors. For example, if an analysis favors mandatory seatbelt legislation, it should discuss such alternatives as requiring air bags or spending more money on safety education.

3. *Assess the desirable and undesirable consequences of the prescription and the alternatives.* For each prescription suggested, the analyst should consider the good and bad consequences that might result directly or indirectly from the policy. Some attempt should be made to weigh the pluses and minuses for each policy and to come up with a conclusion about why the favored prescription is preferred. For example, a mandatory seatbelt law may reduce traffic fatalities, but it may have the undesirable consequence of limiting individual freedom. An air bag law might reduce fatalities even more, but would be much more costly.

EXAMPLE

EXERCISE 3.5: PRESCRIBING PUBLIC POLICY

(A) IDENTIFY AN EXAMPLE OF PRESCRIBING A PUBLIC POLICY EXPRESSED IN THE EDITORIAL EITHER BY QUOTING DIRECTLY FROM THE EDITORIAL OR PARAPHRASING WHAT WAS SAID OR IMPLIED:

An increase in funding of $35 million is requested to fund "agents" who will go out in the streets to seek mentally ill homeless people for treatment in community care centers.

(B) CRITIQUE THE PRESCRIBING OF PUBLIC POLICY. INDICATE BOTH THE STRENGTHS AND WEAKNESSES OF THE ARTICLE BY FOLLOWING THE THREE GUIDELINES POSED IN THE PRECEDING PAGES. NUMBER THE ANSWERS THAT REFER TO EACH GUIDELINE. EITHER GIVE SPECIFIC ILLUSTRATIONS FROM THE EDITORIAL OR SUGGEST HOW THE WRITER MIGHT HAVE SATISFIED THE GUIDELINES PROVIDED:

1. The author provides a clear and specific prescription by endorsing the proposal calling for a corps of 500 case managers to seek out mentally ill people who are on the streets.

2. No alternatives to the policy proposal are mentioned. The author could have considered policies such as reversing the deinstitutionalization process and building more mental institutions.

3. Since no alternatives to the proposed policy are mentioned, the author could not have weighed the relative costs and benefits with the policy proposal. Nevertheless, the treatment of the costs and benefits of the proposal is sketchy. Concerning monetary costs of the policy, the editorial implies that the outreach feature of the proposal will help to prevent some mentally ill persons from becoming homeless. Ignored, however, are the costs of training case workers, the questions of case workers' safety, as well as the benefit of providing more jobs for case workers.

41

SUMMARY

TYPES OF ANALYSIS	DEFINITIONS	CRITICAL FACTORS	EXAMPLES
Monitoring Social Conditions	Describing conditions	Clarity and precision Completeness Quality of evidence	Inflation in the United States was 4% in 1984
Explaining Social Conditions	Providing reasons for past conditions	Multiple factors Reference to authority	More unemployment leads to more crime
Forecasting Social Conditions	Projecting conditions into the future	State time frame Reference to authority Clear reasoning	Crime is expected to increase in the late 1980s
Evaluating Social Conditions	Applying goals to determine whether social conditions are desirable or undesirable	Clearly identified major goals Acknowledgement of other goals	There are too many automobile fatalities in the United States
Prescribing Public Policies	Suggested public policies to create preferred social conditions	Clarity of prescription Reference to alternatives Awareness of potential impact	Raise the drinking age to 21

PART II: INFORMATION-GATHERING SKILLS

In Part I, you took the basic steps toward acquiring effective public policy skills. Now in Part II, you increase your store of knowledge with research and information gathering. Chapter 4 takes you step by step through exercises that help you develop essential library research skills. After completing these exercises, you will find the library a much more understandable resource. Chapters 5 and 6 help you develop tool necessary to get valuable information from the players in public policy.

Chapter 4: Using the Library

Step 1: Selecting Your Topic

Step 2: Defining with Dictionaries and Encyclopedias

Step 3: Collecting Quantitative Data with Almanacs, Yearbooks, and Statistical Sources

Step 4: Gathering Information on Events from Newspapers and Surveys of Events

Step 5: Locating Books

Step 6: Researching through Indexes and Abstracts

Step 7: Using Microforms

Step 8: Using United States Government Publications

Step 9: Using United States Census Data

Chapter 5: Using Surveys

Step 1: Determining the Purpose of a Survey

Step 2: Choosing a Sample

Step 3: Deciding on a Method of Contact

Step 4: Creating the Questions

Step 5: Estimating the Costs of a Survey or Interview

Chapter 6: Gathering Information from Knowledgeable People

Step 1: Preparing for the Interview

Step 2: Locating Knowledgeable People to Interview

Step 3: Gathering Detailed and Accurate Information

CHAPTER 4

USING THE LIBRARY

YOUR GOAL

To locate information related to public policy issues in dictionaries, encyclopedias, journals, magazines, newspapers, microfilm, statistical sources, government publications, books, and other library resources.

INTRODUCTION

To use the library effectively, you need to know what kind of information you need and be able to locate that information quickly. The first task is much more difficult to accomplish than the second. It requires you to know your topic, examine it, and form questions that need to be answered.

You may find some of the tools described in this chapter more useful and available to you than others. Using your school library, complete the following exercises, even if it is not possible to complete all of those in this chapter:

1. Exercise 4.1– in which you identify a public policy issue you would like to study.

2. Exercise 4.2 – in which you use dictionaries and encyclopedias.

3. Exercise 4.4 – in which you use a newspaper index to locate news stories for basic background information.

4. Exercise 4.5 – in which you locate books related to your topic.

5. Exercise 4.8 – in which you use a government catalogue to locate government publications relevant to your topic.

6. Exercise 4.9 – in which you locate U.S. census information.

44

CITATIONS

Always cite the source from which information is taken. If the credit is not given to the source, the material is said to be plagiarized. There are specific forms in which sources should be cited. The style is different for books, magazines, and various other types of sources. Generally, citations should include:

> Author
> Title
> Title of larger work (if part of one)
> Volume number
> Place of publication
> Publishing company
> Year of publication
> Page number
> Any other information necessary to find the material

Below are examples of some of the different styles of citation. Refer to *A Manual for Writers of Term Papers, Theses, and Dissertations* by Kate L. Turabian for the correct way to cite other sources.

Examples of Citations

BOOK

Goode, Richard B. Options for Tax Reform: Papers. Washington D.C.: Brookings Institution, 1984.

YEARBOOK

United Nations. Statistical Yearbook, 1980. New York: United Nations Publications, 1980.

MAGAZINE AND NEWSPAPER ARTICLES

Anderson, Harry. "Mexico Busts Its Top Cops." Newsweek, April 22, 1985, p. 34.

"Mental Health on the Street," New York Times, Monday, January 29, 1988 p. A20.

GOVERNMENT PUBLICATION

U. S. Department of Commerce, Bureau of the Census. Statistical Abstract of the United States, Washington, D.C.: Government Printing Office, 1984.

SOURCE: Turabian, Kate L. A Manual for Writers of Term Papers, Theses, and Dissertations. Chicago: The University of Chicago Press, 1973.

STEP 4.1
SELECTING YOUR TOPIC

Selecting the public policy issue on which to develop library research skills should be done carefully. Ask yourself the following:

1. Do I have some knowledge and interest in the topic?

2. Can I think of other terms that describe or relate to my topic?

3. Can I think of any measurable data related to my topic?

4. Has there been anything in the news concerning my topic?

Did you answer "YES" to all four questions? If not, pick another topic.

EXAMPLE

EXERCISE 4.1: SELECTING YOUR TOPIC

PROVIDE THE REQUESTED INFORMATION:

TOPIC: Housing for homeless people

WHY YOU ARE INTERESTED: I am upset over the growing number of homeless people.

ONE TERM RELATED TO THE TOPIC
(OTHER THAN THE TERM USED IN
YOUR DESCRIPTION OF THE TOPIC): Social Welfare

ONE RELEVANT QUANTITATIVE
INDICATOR: Number of people receiving temporary shelter in New York City (annually)

ONE ACTUAL OR HYPOTHETICAL
NEWSWORTHY EVENT: Mitch Snyder fasts to protest the Reagan Administration's policies on the homeless

ONE ACTUAL OR POSSIBLE
POLICY RELATED TO THE TOPIC: Creating additional shelters for homeless people in New York City

ONE SOCIAL CONDITION
RELATED TO THE TOPIC: Many homeless people die from exposure after sleeping on the streets

ONE PLAYER RELATED TO
THE TOPIC: Director of the Department of Housing and Urban Development

STEP 4.2
DEFINING WITH DICTIONARIES
AND ENCYCLOPEDIAS

The first step in research is to clearly define what you are studying. Definitions can be found in dictionaries and encyclopedias. A dictionary provides the range of meanings people usually attach to important terms related to your public policy issue. Historical background information on major events and conditions that shape the issue are found in an encyclopedia.

A list of dictionaries and encyclopedias that you might use includes:

DICTIONARIES

The Oxford English Dictionary. 13 vols. New York: Oxford University Press, 1933 (with supplements).

Webster's Third New International Dictionary. Springfield, Massachusetts: Merriam - Webster, 1981.

Reading, Hugo. Dictionary of the Social Sciences. Boston: Routledge and Kegan Paul, 1977.

The Random House Dictionary of the English Language. New York: Random House, 1968.

ENCYCLOPEDIAS

Encyclopaedia Britannica. Chicago: Encyclopedia Britannica Educational Corporation, 1985. This 32-volume work was recently revised in an attempt to make it easier to use.

Encyclopedia Americana. Danbury, Connecticut: Grolier Educational Corporation, 1983. Another 30-volume set which is particularly good for information on towns and cities.

Use your library's online catalog or card catalog to locate each source.

48

EXAMPLE

EXERCISE 4.2: DEFINING WITH DICTIONARIES AND ENCYCLOPEDIAS

FIND AND DEFINE TWO TERMS THAT ARE RELATED TO YOUR TOPIC AND COMPLETE THE FOLLOWING OUTLINE. (PAY SPECIAL ATTENTION TO THE FORM OF THE CITATION AND FOLLOW IT EXACTLY AS IT APPEARS IN THE EXAMPLE EXERCISE.):

TERM 1: Homeless

DEFINITION: 1) without a home, 2) affording no home

CITATION OF GENERAL
DICTIONARY USED: The Random House Dictionary of the English Language,
College Edition. New York: Random House, 1968.

PAGE NUMBER: 633

TERM 2: Social Welfare

DEFINITION: Various institutions and services whose primary purpose is to maintain and enhance the physical, social, intellectual, or emotional well-being of people.

CITATION OF GENERAL
ENCYCLOPEDIA: Encyclopedia Americana. Danbury, Connecticut: Grolier Educational Corporation, 1983.

PAGE NUMBER: 139

STEP 4.3
COLLECTING QUANTITATIVE DATA WITH ALMANACS, YEARBOOKS, AND STATISTICAL SOURCES

Almanacs and yearbooks give both statistical and general descriptive information in an easy to find format. Here is a brief list of some of the more widely used sources.

ALMANACS

Information Please Almanac. New York: Simon and Schuster, 1947-.

The World Almanac and Book of Facts. New York: Newspaper Enterprise Association, 1868-.

YEARBOOKS

The County Year Book. Washington, D.C.: International City Management Association, 1975-.

The Municipal Year Book. Washington, D.C.: International City Management Association, 1948-.

The Statesman's Year-Book. New York: St. Martin's Press, 1964-.

OTHER STATISTICAL SOURCES

U. S. Department of Commerce. Bureau of the Census. City Government Finances, 1909-.

U. S. Department of Commerce. Bureau of the Census. County and City Data Book, 1949-.

American Statistics Index. Washington, D.C.: Congressional Information Service, 1973-.

U. S. Department of Census. Statistical Abstract of the United States, Washington, D.C.: Government Printing Office, 1879–.

The *American Statistics Index* (ASI) cited above is a particularly useful source because it assists in finding statistics that appear in the thousands of government publications published each year. Because it is such an important source, we will provide detailed information here on how to use it. The ASI is published in two parts for each year: Index and Abstracts. The Index provides information by subjects, authors (which may be individuals or agencies), and categories: the Abstracts provide bibliographic data, descriptions of the subject matter, and outlines of content with references to specific page ranges. Here are the four steps to follow in using ASI:

1. Search the Index to identify publications of interest.

2. Note the accession numbers.

3. Use the accession number to locate and review the abstracts in the ASI Abstracts volume for information on the contents of the publications. (The most current year will be in paper form as an unbound supplement.)

4. Obtain the publications for complete reference.

EXAMPLE

EXERCISE 4.3: COLLECTING QUANTITATIVE DATA WITH ALMANACS, YEARBOOKS, AND STATISTICAL SOURCES

(A) USING AN ALMANAC, LOOK THROUGH THE TABLE OF CONTENTS OR THE INDEX FOR TERMS RELEVANT TO YOUR TOPIC. FIND ONE STATISTIC RELEVANT TO YOUR SUBJECT. DO NOT LOOK FOR THE PERFECT STATISTIC, JUST ONE THAT HAS SOME RELEVANCE. CITE THE ALMANAC, DEFINE THE STATISTIC CLEARLY, AND RECORD THE FIGURE PROVIDED. (PAY SPECIAL ATTENTION TO THE FORM OF THE CITATION AND FOLLOW IT EXACTLY AS IT APPEARS IN THE EXAMPLE EXERCISE.):

CITATION: The World Almanac and Book of Facts. New York: Newspaper Enterprise Association, 1984.

STATISTIC DEFINITION: U.S. Budget outlay to Housing and Urban Development Department for fiscal 1982

FIGURE: $144.91 billion

(B) USING A YEARBOOK OR OTHER STATISTICAL SOURCE (EXCLUDING ALMANACS) LOOK THROUGH THE TABLE OF CONTENTS OR THE INDEX FOR TERMS RELEVANT TO YOUR TOPIC. FIND ONE STATISTIC RELEVANT TO YOUR SUBJECT. DO NOT LOOK FOR THE PERFECT STATISTIC, JUST ONE THAT HAS SOME RELEVANCE. CITE THE SOURCE, INCLUDING THE PAGE ON WHICH THE STATISTIC IS FOUND, AND DEFINE THE STATISTIC CLEARLY. (PAY SPECIAL ATTENTION TO THE FORM OF THE CITATION AND FOLLOW IT EXACTLY AS IT APPEARS IN THE EXAMPLE EXERCISE.):

CITATION: U.S. Department of Commerce, Bureau of the Census. City Government Finances, 1982-83, p.263.

STATISTIC DEFINITION: Percentage distribution of city government finances to Housing and Community Development, for municipalities of 1,000,000 or more as of 1980, for fiscal 1982-83

FIGURE: 35.9%

(C) USING THE AMERICAN STATISTICS INDEX (ASI), IDENTIFY ONE STATISTIC RELEVANT TO YOUR SUBJECT. USE THE ASI'S INDEX TO FIND THE SOURCE OF A STATISTIC; RECORD THE DATE OF THE ASI YOU USE AND THE PUBLICATION'S ACCESS NUMBER; FIND THE ABSTRACT IN THE ASI ABSTRACT VOLUME; AND PROVIDE A DEFINITION OF THE STATISTIC. ALSO, INDICATE THE TITLE AND AUTHOR OF THE PUBLICATION.

ASI INDEX DATE: October-December 1977

PUBLICATION ACCESS NUMBER: 7888-21

TITLE AND AUTHOR OF PUBLICATION: Keith M. Goodman and Melinda A. Green, "Low-Fare and Fare-Free Transit: Some Recent Applications by United States Transit System"

DESCRIPTION OF THE STATISTIC: Statistics on mass-transit ridership in 41 large cities

52

STEP 4.4
GATHERING INFORMATION ON EVENTS FROM NEWSPAPERS AND SURVEYS OF EVENTS

Every library subscribes to at least one newspaper, and most subscribe to several. The larger national newspapers have indexes which allow you to locate events about your topic.

An **event** is one of two things: (1) It may be an action at a specific time and place by an identifiable person, group, or institution. A speech or passage of a law is a common event that affects policy. Policies and social conditions are not events. For example, the passage of a mandatory seatbelt law is an event, but the existence of the law or its effect on traffic fatalities is not an event. The unemployment rate in the United States is not an event, but it is an event if the President announces the current unemployment rate. (2) An event may be a physical occurrence at a particular time and place, such as a hurricane or earthquake.

Surveys of events provide information on recent happenings. These sources tend to give more information than newspapers, and often include some background information on the topic.

NEWSPAPER INDEXES

New York Times Index. New York: New York Times, 1913–.

Christian Science Monitor Subject Index. Boston: Christian Science Publishing Society, 1960-.

Wall Street Journal Index. New York: Dow Jones Company, 1958-.

SURVEYS OF EVENTS

Congressional Quarterly Weekly Report. Washington, D.C.: Congressional Quarterly, 1945-.

Facts on File. New York: Facts on File, 1940-.

Keesing's Contemporary Archives. London: Kessing's, 1931-.

EXAMPLE

EXERCISE 4.4: GATHERING INFORMATION ON EVENTS FROM NEWSPAPERS AND SURVEYS OF EVENTS

(A) USING THE <u>NEW YORK TIMES INDEX</u>, FIND A REFERENCE TO ONE MAJOR EVENT. RECORD THE PAGE NUMBER OF THE TIMES ARTICLE. (PAY SPECIAL ATTENTION TO THE FORM OF THE CITATION AND FOLLOW IT EXACTLY AS IT APPEARS IN THE EXAMPLE EXERCISE.):

EVENT: House of Representatives Democratic leaders unanimously commit themselves to an Emergency Economic Assistance Program

DATE: 2/2/83
PAGE NO.: A1

SOURCE CITATION: <u>New York Times Index</u>. New York: New York Times, 1984.

(B) NEXT, LOOK UP THE SAME EVENT IN A SURVEY OF EVENTS. RECORD THE DATE AND PAGE NUMBER OF THESE ARTICLES. (PAY SPECIAL ATTENTION TO THE FORM OF THE CITATION AND FOLLOW IT EXACTLY AS IT APPEARS IN THE EXAMPLE EXERCISE.) OTHER SOURCES MAY NOT HAVE REPORTED THE EVENT ON THE SAME DATES AS THE NEW YORK TIMES. THEREFORE, CHECK YOUR OTHER SOURCE FOR ONE WEEK PRECEDING AND FOLLOWING THE NEW YORK TIMES PUBLICATION DATE. IF THE EVENT DOES NOT APPEAR IN THE SOURCE, INDICATE THE RANGE OF DAYS YOU ACTUALLY CHECKED:

SOURCE TITLE: <u>Facts on File</u>   DATE: 2/4/83
                                          PAGE NO.:   70

SOURCE CITATION: <u>Facts on File</u>, New York: Facts on File, Volume 43, No. 2203, 1983.

STEP 4.5
LOCATING BOOKS

Although much of the information required for research can be found in journals and newspapers, you often need in-depth, detailed information which can only be found in books. By becoming more familiar with the system of organization in your library, the job of locating books becomes much easier. Books are found on shelves by number. These are **call numbers**. Most libraries use one of two major coding systems for organizing a library collection: the Library of Congress System or the Dewey Decimal System. Under both these systems, the call numbers group materials by subjects. A different call number is assigned to each item in the library. Once books are coded, information on them is filed either in a card catalog or, increasingly, in a computer-based system.

Under the Library of Congress System, the books are coded by a combination of numbers and letters. The first letter (or first two letters) denotes the subject heading. The classifications are:

A	General Works	M	Music
B	Philosophy and Religion	N	Fine Arts
C	Auxiliary Sciences of History	P	Philosophy, Language and
D	General Old World and Eastern		Literature
	European History	Q	Science
E-F	American History	R	Medicine
G	Geography and Anthropology	S	Agriculture
H	Social Sciences	T	Technology
J	Political Science	U	Military Science
K	Law	V	Naval Science
L	Education	W	Bibliography and Library Science

The Dewey Decimal System divides all books into 10 major categories each bearing a number. The major divisions are:

000-General Works	600-Technology (Applied Sciences)
100-Philosophy and Related Disciplines	700-The Arts
200-Religion	800-Literature and Rhetoric
300-The Social Sciences	900-General Geography and History
400-Languages	and Their Auxiliaries
500-Pure Sciences	(including Biography)

Each of the Dewey Decimal System categories can be divided into 10 more subdivisions. Since we are primarily dealing with Social Sciences, it is useful to know how the Dewey System breaks down the Social Sciences (300) category:

300-General	350-Public Administration
310-Statistics	360-Welfare
320-Political Science	370-Education
330-Economics	380-Commerce
340-Law	390-Customs and Folklore

The call number begins with the letter (Library of Congress) or the number (Dewey System) assigned to the book's general classification and then continues with further coding to more narrowly define the book. The card catalog generally contains at least three cards for every book—a title card, an author card, and a subject card. For the most part, these cards contain the same information, but are filed differently in the alphabetically ordered catalog.

Each card contains information on the title, author, editor, place and date of publication, number of pages, size, contents, call number, and tracings. The tracings indicate other subject headings under which this book is located, and can also lead to additional titles on the same subject. Some books have tracings on all three cards, but others list tracings only on the author card.

The card catalog will be one of two types: divided or non-divided. The divided catalog will have the author and title cards in the same file, with the subject cards filed separately. The non-divided catalog will have all three types of cards indexed together in the same file.

Computer search systems provide more rapid and varied procedures for finding books. Most systems are organized around the same categories as the card catalog. In addition, some systems allow you to find a book, if you know the call number. If you know only two or three words in the title, it may tell you the exact title. Check the information on the computer system in your library carefully. You will find it more efficient than the card catalog for most searches.

The best place to begin a search is under the subject. If you cannot find a related subject listed in the card catalog or search system, check the *Library of Congress List of Subject Headings*. This is a guide to subject headings used in college and university libraries throughout the country. The list not only provides subject headings which may be used, but also includes cross-references to other terms.

Example:

Discrimination in Employment (Indirect)
(HD4903)

sa   Affirmative action programs
Age and employment
Blacklisting, labor
Equal pay for equal work
Sex discrimination in employment
Trade unions—minority membership subdivision
Employment under names of racial or social groups, e.g., Afro-
Americans—Employment; Women—Employment

x   Employment discrimination
Equal employment opportunity
Equal opportunity in employment
Fair employment practices
Job discrimination

xx   Discrimination
Labor and laboring classes
Personnel management
Race discrimination
Right to labor
Trade unions—minority membership
Labor laws and legislation

—   Law and legislation (Indirect)

Discrimination in Employment is a subject heading. The letters *sa* indicate more specific headings or related terms which may also be used (*Equal pay for equal work; Women—Employment*). The letter *x* indicates terms which are not used as subject headings. The letters *xx* indicate terms which are used, but which are much broader terms. The symbol — indicates a subdivision or more specific term. In the example above, *Discrimination in employment—Law and legislation* is also a subject heading that can be used.

Finally, there are *See* references. For example, *Labor unions see Trade unions* indicates that material about labor unions will be located under the subject heading *Trade unions*.

Once you have identified the book you want in the card catalog or computer search system, note its call number and locate it on the shelf. Books are arranged on the shelves numerically in the Dewey Decimal System and alphabetically in the Library of Congress System.

EXAMPLE

EXERCISE 4.5: LOCATING BOOKS

(A) LIST TWO ENTRIES YOU USED TO FIND BOOKS ON YOUR SUBJECT, USING THE COMPUTER SEARCH SYSTEM IN YOUR LIBRARY. (IF YOUR LIBRARY DOES NOT HAVE A COMPUTER SEARCH SYSTEM, USE THE CARD CATALOG.):

SEARCH CODE AND WORDS OR TOPIC HEADINGS: SB: Homeless
SB: Public Housing

(B) OBTAIN TWO BOOKS THAT YOU FOUND THROUGH YOUR SEARCH, PROVIDE A COMPLETE CITATION, AND WRITE A BRIEF SUMMARY ABOUT THE BOOK. (PAY SPECIAL ATTENTION TO THE FORM OF THE CITATION AND FOLLOW IT EXACTLY AS IT APPEARS IN THE EXAMPLE EXERCISE.):

CITATION 1: Cuomo, Mario Matthew. <u>Forest Hills Diary</u>. New York: Vintage Books, 1983.

SUMMARY: In 1972, New York City proposed to build a low-income housing project in Forest Hills. The area is a middle-class, middle-income neighborhood in Queens. A lawyer, Mario Cuomo, was assigned by the mayor to mediate the dispute that arose. This book is a day-by-day diary of the proceedings in which Cuomo offers insight into the cause of the crisis, the ongoing conflict, and the effects of possible resolutions.

CITATION 2: Erickson, Jon and Wilhelm, Charles, eds. <u>Housing the Homeless</u>. Rutgers State University of New Jersey: Center for Urban Policy Research, 1986.

SUMMARY: This book contains 31 articles contributed by government agencies, professors, newswriters, and others connected with the issue of the homeless. The book describes the perception America has of the homeless and how and why the homeless became homeless. Also examined are the resources available to aid the homeless, possible solutions to the problem, and the significance of the number of homeless people. There are also articles discussing the homeless as a political issue and the book provides background to the general problem.

STEP 4.6
RESEARCHING THROUGH INDEXES AND ABSTRACTS

Now that you have clarified your topic, you are ready to begin researching it. For current public policy issues, valuable sources of information are found in magazines and journal articles—referred to as *periodical literature.*

Magazine and journal articles can be used to provide both background information and more information on the current status of your public policy issue. Magazines and journals differ in several respects. Magazines have more readers and carry extensive advertising. Magazine articles tend to cover the activities of players on a public policy issue and the possible impact of new public policies. Journals are designed for scholars, analysts, and players in the policy-making process. Journal articles tend to cover social conditions prompting public policies and to provide thorough bibliographic citations. They are published less frequently than magazines. Articles must undergo a review process that involves evaluations by specialists in the field. Journal articles usually have less current information than magazine articles.

Because many articles are published every year, you need some way to search systematically for those articles that are appropriate to your topic. This is done by abstracting and indexing services. These sources list articles, most often by subject, and provide the article title, author, journal name, date, issue, volume, and page number.

There are four kinds of indexes:

1. *General Indexes:* These cover a large number of periodicals on a variety of subjects.

2. *Subject Indexes:* These cover a large number of periodicals on single general topics such as business, public administration, etc.

3. *Single Title Indexes:* These cover only one publication or title.

4. *Abstracts:* These provide, in addition to index information, brief summaries of the articles.

The information in indexes is arranged alphabetically by subject, and occasionally by author as well, and sometimes by title. Since it is likely that you will be conducting a search by subject, you will be faced with the problem of what subject heading to look up. Think of several different terms to describe important aspects of your topic.

For instance, if you were looking for articles on world hunger, you might come up with such terms as hunger, food supplies, famine, and drought. These could also lead you to related terms like desertification, rainfall, climate, and weather. Once you have thought of six to ten terms, look through the subject headings in the indexing or abstracting service to see if any of those words appear. If they do not, you will have to think of other terms used by the service that are relevant to your topic.

Indexes can be found to cover almost any area of interest. For public policy analysis, however, certain indexes and abstracts are most useful. Many of them are listed below. Note that the *Readers' Guide to Periodical Literature* is identified as a general index because it covers all areas, not just the social sciences. The others are focused more directly on the social sciences and, therefore, are relevant to a wide range of public policy issues. Also, the *Readers' Guide* indexes magazine articles, while the subject indexes and abstracts cover primarily journal articles.

GENERAL INDEXES

Readers' Guide to Periodical Literature. New York: H. W. Wilson Company, 1900-. A comprehensive guide to non-technical journals. About 169 periodicals are catalogued.

SUBJECT INDEXES

Bulletin of the Public Affairs Information Service (PAIS). New York: PAIS, 1916-. A subject index to current literature on economic and social conditions.

Index of Economic Articles in Journals and Collective Volumes. Homewood, Illinois: R.D. Irwin Company, 1961-. An index of articles from about 140 sources from various countries.

Social Sciences Index. New York: H.W. Wilson Company, 1974-. An index to more than 200 periodicals in the various fields of the social sciences.

Social Sciences Citation Index. Philadelphia: Institute for Scientific Information, 1973-. An international interdisciplinary index to the literature of the social sciences.

ABSTRACTS

Criminal Justice Abstracts. Monsey, New York: Will Tree Press, 1968-. (Formerly Crime and Delinquency Literature.) Contains abstracts of the current books, journal articles, and reports in the field of crime and criminal justice.

Human Resources Abstracts. Beverly Hills, California: Sage Publications, 1975-. Covers material related to social and labor problems, (Formerly Poverty and Human Resources Abstracts.)

International Political Science Abstracts. Paris: International Political Science Association, 1951-. Covers articles published in many countries in the field of political science.

Women's Studies Abstracts. Rush, New York: Rush Publishing Company, 1972-. Contains abstracts from a wide range of periodicals dealing with topics concerning women.

EXAMPLE

EXERCISE 4.6: RESEARCHING THROUGH INDEXES AND ABSTRACTS

(A) USING THE <u>READERS' GUIDE TO PERIODICAL LITERATURE</u>, LIST TWO SUBJECT HEADINGS WHICH COULD BE USED IN LOCATING ARTICLES RELEVANT TO YOUR TOPIC. FIND ONE RELEVANT ARTICLE, GIVE A FULL CITATION, AND WRITE A SUMMARY (AT LEAST 30 WORDS) OF THE ARTICLE. (PAY SPECIAL ATTENTION TO THE FORM OF THE CITATION AND FOLLOW IT EXACTLY AS IT APPEARS IN THE EXAMPLE EXERCISE.):

INDEX OR ABSTRACT
CITATION: <u>Readers' Guide to Periodical Literature</u>. Vol.43. New York: H.W. Wilson Company, February 1984.

SUBJECT HEADING #1: Housing

SUBJECT HEADING #2: U.S. Department of Housing and Urban Development

ARTICLE CITATION: Kinsley, M. "Who's the Fairest of Them All?" <u>Harper's</u>, January 1983, p. 6.

SUMMARY: The article discusses federal housing programs and changes in the programs over the past two decades. The author discusses the unfairness of the Reagan administration's policies. The author also states that while the homeless are helped in a random and inefficient manner, they would not be better off without it.

(B) SELECT ONE OF THE INDEXES OR ABSTRACTS LISTED IN THE PREVIOUS TWO PAGES OTHER THAN THE READERS' GUIDE, GIVE A FULL CITATION OF THE INDEX OR ABSTRACT, AND LIST TWO SUBJECT HEADINGS THAT COULD BE USED IN LOCATING ARTICLES RELEVANT TO YOUR TOPIC. FIND ONE RELEVANT ARTICLE, GIVE A FULL CITATION, AND A SUMMARY (AT LEAST 30 WORDS) OF THE ARTICLE:

INDEX OR ABSTRACT
CITATION: <u>Human Resources Abstract</u>. Vol. 18, No.4. Beverly Hills, California: Sage Publications, December 1983.

SUBJECT HEADING #1: Public Housing

SUBJECT HEADING #2: Poverty

ARTICLE CITATION: Vitaliana, D.F. "Public Housing and Slums: Cure or Cause?" <u>Urban Studies</u> 20 (May 1983): 173.

SUMMARY: The author uses U.S. Census data to estimate the effect public housing has on private renting in 33 cities. The results show a 6-9% decrease in private rentals for every one percent increase in the proportion of public housing in the total housing.

(continued)

61

EXAMPLE

EXERCISE 4.6: (continued)

(C)   USING INFOTRAC OR SOME OTHER ON-LINE JOURNAL INDEX SERVICE, PRINT OUT
AND PASTE IN THE SPACE PROVIDED BELOW TWO CITATIONS RELATED TO YOUR
TOPIC.

HOMELESSNESS
–ANALYSIS
      Why Are They Homeless? (In the Cities) by Peter Marcuse il Nation v244-April 4'87
   p426(3)

HOMELESSNESS
–CAUSES OF
      Where Do the Homeless Come From? (includes three related articles) by William
   Tucker il National Review v39-Sept 25 '87 p32(7)

STEP 4.7
USING MICROFORMS

In order to save space, back issues of many newspapers, some periodicals, and numerous United States government and international documents are put on microforms. This process makes it possible for a library to hold more past issues. There is also less worry about decay or destruction of the printed material through age or constant use. There are several types of microforms, of which the most frequently used are:

- *Microfilm*: Microfilm is a reel of film, usually 100 feet (30m) long and 16mm or 35mm in width, containing photographic records of the material. It is the standard format for backruns of journals and newspapers.

- *Microfiche*: Microfiche is a piece of film, usually 4 by 6 inches, containing either 60 or 98 frames or pictures on a card in a grid pattern.

EXAMPLE

EXERCISE 4.7: USING MICROFORMS

USING A NEWSPAPER INDEX SUCH AS THE NEW YORK TIMES INDEX, LOCATE AN ARTICLE ON A MICROFORM THAT PROVIDES EITHER HISTORICAL OR GENERAL BACKGROUND INFORMATION ON YOUR TOPIC. (A) COMPLETE THE CITATION FOR THE ARTICLE. (B) HAVE THE ARTICLE REPRODUCED ON PAPER AND ATTACH IT TO THIS PAGE:

(A) CITATION: "Warm Season Masks but Doesn't End Problems of the Homeless." <u>New York Times</u>, June 3, 1983, p. A16.

(B)

Warm Season Masks but Doesn't End Problems of the Homeless

STEP 4.8
USING UNITED STATES GOVERNMENT PUBLICATIONS

Every year the United States government publishes thousands of pages of material on many different subjects. These materials can be very valuable in studying public policy issues.

Perhaps the most important publication in this category is the *Monthly Catalog of United States Government Publications*. There are several search strategies that can be employed in locating the government publications that might be helpful. The most frequently used approach is to check the subject index of the *Monthly Catalog*. There is also a title index if you already know the title of the publication for which you are looking. As a last resort, you may want to refer to the author index. If you are aware of the government agency associated with the topic, you can refer to the author index in the back of the Monthly Catalog. The index will provide you with an entry number which you then use to locate the full entry or bibliographic citation.

Among other details, each entry in the *Monthly Catalog* gives the entry number, the author, the title, the date, and the Superintendent of Documents (Su-Doc) number.

Documents may be arranged in the school library in two ways—either cataloged by government author and shelved along with other books, or arranged according to Su-Doc number and cataloged by the *Monthly Catalog*. Consult the librarian on how the collection is organized.

Should more information on government documents be needed, read Joe Morehead's *Introduction to United States Public Documents* (3rd ed.), Littleton, Colorado: Libraries Unlimited, 1983.

EXAMPLE

EXERCISE 4.8: USING UNITED STATES GOVERNMENT PUBLICATIONS

USING THE *MONTHLY CATALOG OF UNITED STATES GOVERNMENT PUBLICATIONS*, LO-CATE TWO PUBLICATIONS RELEVANT TO YOUR TOPIC AND GIVE THE ENTRY NUMBER, THE TITLE, THE ISSUING AGENCY, AND THE SU-DOC NUMBER.

PUBLICATION 1:

ENTRY NUMBER: 84-4198

TITLE: Efforts to Reduce Taxpayer Burdens

AGENCY: Committee on Finance, United States Senate

SU-DOC NUMBER: Y4.F 49:5.hrg.98-197

PUBLICATION 2:

ENTRY NUMBER: 84-14039

TITLE: Tax Law and Simplification Act of 1983

AGENCY: Committee on Ways and Means, House of Representatives

SU-DOC NUMBER: Y4.W 36:98-40

66

STEP 4.9
USING UNITED STATES CENSUS DATA

A special type of government document is published by the United States Bureau of the Census. Every 10 years the Bureau collects information on population and housing for the entire country. This information is updated within the 10 year period through estimates and sample surveys.

The Census Bureau breaks the nation down in several ways. These are:

1. *Regions/Division:* There are four census regions (west, south, northeast, and north central) defined by the United States Census Bureau, each composed of two or more divisions. Divisions are areas composed of groupings of contiguous states.

2. *Standard Metropolitan Statistical Areas (SMSAs):* In 1970 an SMSA comprised a county containing a central city (or twin cities) of 50,000 or more, plus contiguous counties which were socially and economically integrated with the central county. All counties in SMSAs are termed "metropolitan," and all others "nonmetropolitan."

3. *Urbanized Areas (UAs):* UAs comprise a central city of an SMSA, plus the surrounding, closely-settled urban fringe ("suburbs").

4. *Urban/Rural:* The urban population comprises all persons living in urbanized areas and in places of 2,500 or more outside urbanized areas. Everyone else is considered rural.

5. *Unincorporated Places:* A concentration of population which is not legally incorporated. Suitable boundaries are defined for statistical purposes by the Census Bureau with local assistance. Unincorporated places of less than 1,000 inhabitants are disregarded.

6. *Census Tracts:* Subdivisions of SMSAs averaging 4,000 population, covering all SMSAs for 1970. Tracts are defined by local committees and are frequently used to approximate neighborhoods.

7. *Enumeration Districts (EDs):* Administrative divisions set up by the Census Bureau to take the census in areas where enumerators were used, averaging 800 population. Outside of urbanized areas, this is the smallest geographic unit of analysis, and all other areas such as tracts, places, and MCDs can be defined as a collection of EDs.

8. *Block Groups (BGs):* Groups of city blocks, averaging 1,000 population, which take the place of enumeration districts in 145 large urbanized areas where the census was taken by mail in 1970.

9. *Blocks:* City blocks are areas generally bound by four streets or some other physical boundary, defined in urbanized areas and in additional cities which contracted with the Bureau for collection of block statistics.

67

The Census Bureau gathers information on many items under the two main headings of population and housing. Information includes:

POPULATION ITEMS

- Relationship to head of household

- Color or race

- Age

- Sex

- Marital status

HOUSING ITEMS

- Number of housing units at this address

- Telephone

- Complete kitchen facilities

- Rooms

- Water supply

- Flush toilet

- Bathtub or shower

- Owner/renter

- Commercial establishment on property

- Value

The information gathered is compiled in a series of reports covering a variety of areas and subjects. To find a specific subject the best source is the *1980 Census of Population and Housing Census Tracts*. A general guide to the use of census data is the *Census Catalog and Guide 1987*. Both of these publications are available from the Data User Services Division, United States Bureau of the Census, Washington, D.C. and can be found in many libraries.

EXAMPLE

EXERCISE 4.9: USING UNITED STATES CENSUS DATA

(A) CHOOSE A SMSA (STANDARD METROPOLITAN STATISTICAL AREA) AND INDICATE THE NUMBER ASSIGNED TO IT:

THE SMSA I HAVE CHOSEN IS: Nassau-Suffolk New York   (253)

(B) USING THE 1980 CENSUS TRACT REPORT, LOCATE THE FOLLOWING INFORMATION FOR YOUR SMSA. DATA IS PRESENTED IN A SERIES OF TABLES AND YOU NEED TO FIND THE APPROPRIATE TABLES.

CATEGORY	DATA
TOTAL PERSONS:	2,605,813
PERSONS PER HOUSEHOLD:	3.16
MARRIED COUPLE FAMILIES:	580,006
TOTAL PERSONS OF SPANISH ORIGIN:	101,975
MEDIAN FAMILY INCOME:	$26,242

69

SUMMARY

TYPES OF INFORMATION	RESEARCH TOOLS	EXAMPLES
Definitions	Dictionaries and encyclopedias	Fiscal (pertaining to the public treasury or revenues)
Scholarly and Journalistic Analysis	Indexes, abstracts, card catalogs, and computer search systems for books and articles	*Bulletin of the Public Affairs Information Service (PAIS)*
Statistical Information on Conditions	Almanacs, yearbooks, and other statistical sources	Number of automobile fatalities in the U.S.
Information on Events	Newspaper indexes, surveys of events,and microforms	Congressional budget officers urge Congress to raise taxes, 2/11/83
Government Information	*Monthly Catalog,* Census Publications	"Background on Federal Income Tax Compliance"

PARTICIPATION ACTIVITY: Providing Library Research to Players

1. Select a policy issue that you (or your group) would be interested in studying.

2. Identify a specific player that is interested in the selected issue. Contact the player directly by phone or mail. If you are not sure how to identify and locate the player, review Chapter 6, which provides the necessary information. If you have trouble contacting the actual player or one of the player's assistants, you can still undertake the project and submit it without prior contact. However, it is better to get help from the player at the outset. If you are unable to arrange a meeting, skip the next step and go directly to 4.

3. Explain that you would like to provide the player with an annotated bibliography or research report based on library research on the issue. Ask for suggestions on types of information you might pursue and leads on where you might find the information.

4. Using the guidelines provided in this chapter, prepare an annotated bibliography or research report on material in the library that might be of interest to the player or, provide the actual information that player requires. End your report with suggestions of other leads that the player might follow (for example, a reference book at a near-by university library).

5. Complete the report on the agreed-upon date, submit it in written form, and offer to make an oral presentation.

6. Thank the player for the opportunity to provide the service. Provide a report to the class on your experience.

CHAPTER 5

USING SURVEYS

YOUR GOAL

To define the purpose, select the sample, write the questions, plan the method of contact, and estimate the costs for a survey.

INTRODUCTION

Surveys can be a vital source of information for the study of current public policy issues. They can range in form from open-ended interviews of a few key public officials to a mail survey of thousands of people. They provide more up-to-date information than is usually available in print form. This chapter introduces you to the basic principles of survey design.

STEP 5.1
DETERMINING THE PURPOSE OF A SURVEY

Surveys provide information that policy-makers or policy analysts can use in any of the five steps of policy analysis: monitoring, explaining, forecasting, evaluating, and prescribing. When you plan a survey, consider first who will be using the information you gather and for what purpose they want the information. You might, for example, conduct a survey for a government official who wants to assess the impact of a policy, or for a pressure group hoping to use the results to support its views. By considering for whom the information is to be gathered and for what purpose they hope to use it, you will have a clearer picture of what questions to ask and what people you will need to approach for answers.

All surveys should provide honest, objective information. You should only do surveys for clients willing to allow you to follow objective, careful procedures. The purpose of a survey is not to prove a point, but to determine whether or not a point is provable. For example, a survey should not be conducted to prove that all people feel the seatbelt law deprives them of their liberty; rather, a survey could be conducted to discover how people feel about the seatbelt law. A survey never tells you whether a policy is good or bad, or whether it should or should not be implemented. It only gives you information on conditions or people's attitudes, or their perceptions of facts.

You may obtain factual and attitudinal information with surveys.

- **Factual information** about social conditions and public policies might consist of people's occupations, their incomes, their behavior, their physical environment, or trends in government action. For example, a study of mandatory seatbelt use in New York State might ask people whether or not they personally use seatbelts. The information derived from such a question would indicate how many people use seatbelts.

- **Attitudinal information** indicates how people feel and think about social conditions or about public policies designed to deal with those conditions. In the mandatory seatbelt example, a survey might determine if people feel more secure when they wear seatbelts.

Part of identifying the purpose of the survey is to clearly define the **target population**, the group of people about whom you wish to know more. The most well-known types of surveys are public opinion surveys of a large sample of the population. However, smaller sample surveys of specialized groups are often more useful in policy analysis because key groups of people may be more knowledgeable about policy, or in a better position to influence policy. For example, in a survey of the uses of food stamps, a sample drawn from the users of food stamps would be more appropriate than a sample drawn from the general population.

Even when large-scale surveys are undertaken, as in a pre-election survey, sophisticated pollsters attempt to sample those members of the general population who are most likely to vote. Defining the target population consists of three steps:

1. Determine the approximate size of your target population. This will help you decide on the method of survey and the size of your sample.

2. State the geographic scope of the target population. If the study is about county-wide attitudes toward health care services, it is not enough to study people in a single town. On the other hand, if the study relates to a town's policy, do not use a survey of the outer county.

3. Indicate what age, occupation, sex, or other characteristics might apply to your target population. A study on how food stamps are used, for example, would focus on a sample of those individuals who receive food stamps.

EXAMPLE

EXERCISE 5.1: DETERMINING THE PURPOSE OF A SURVEY

(A) SPECIFY FOR WHOM THE INFORMATION IS BEING GATHERED AND WHAT DECISIONS WILL BE MADE AS A RESULT OF IT:

The information is being gathered for Ms. N. Drew, the principal of Riverdale High School. She feels the school must provide programs to combat the high number of teenage suicides.

(B) INDICATE HOW THE INFORMATION GATHERED IN THE SURVEY WILL BE USED IN ONE OR MORE OF THE FIVE TYPES OF ANALYSIS:

The survey will help forecast the level of student participation in workshops on teenage suicide.

Based on the results of this survey (and other information), the principal will decide whether or not the school should sponsor workshops on teenage suicide. If workshops are planned, the results of the survey will be used to determine the leaders of the workshop.

(C) IDENTIFY THE TARGET POPULATION WHICH YOU WILL SAMPLE FOR YOUR SURVEY (INCLUDING SIZE):

All high school age people, including drop-outs, in Riverdale. This consists of approximately 2000 people.

(D) IDENTIFY WHAT FACTUAL AND ATTITUDINAL INFORMATION YOU WILL GATHER:

Factual: (1) Have teenagers ever attended any type of program on teenage suicide? (2) Have teenagers known teens who have committed suicide or made a suicide attempt?

Attitudinal: (1) Do teenagers think they would benefit from workshops on teenage suicide? (2) Would teenagers prefer to attend workshops conducted by school staff or by experts from the community?

STEP 5.2
CHOOSING A SAMPLE

In choosing a sample, two decisions have to be made: sample size and method of selection. In most cases, it is impossible to survey everyone in the target population. Therefore, it is necessary to select a representative portion of the target population. The goal of a sample is to select a group of subjects whose responses would be representative of the population as a whole.

SAMPLE SIZE

The size of a sample is more important than the percentage of the total population sampled. (This assumes, of course, that the sample was correctly selected.) Accurate samples of the total United States population can consist of as few as 2000 people. A sample of this size represents only about .00001 of the total population, but when correctly selected, can give a highly accurate representation of the entire population. If the population itself is much smaller, a survey must be based on a sample of a much larger proportion of the population in order to keep the actual size large enough so that it can be analyzed properly. In those cases where the target population is less than 50, the survey should include all members of the population. When all members of a population are surveyed, it is called a census. Aside from the size of the target population, the other factor in sample size is the complexity of the analysis to be made of the survey results. If only the number of total responses is of interest (which is rarely the case in policy analysis), then a sample of 100 or even 50 would be adequate. But if a more complex analysis is to be done, such as how different sub-groups of the sample respond, then a sample size of 1000-2000 is required.

The term **sample size** refers to the actual number of responses you receive to your questions, not the number of questionnaires you distribute. If you conduct your survey by mail, this can be a serious problem. Experience with mail surveys indicates a return rate of more than 10% is very rare.

SAMPLE SELECTION

Sampling can be done either through random or non-random methods. In survey research, the word random is used in a very specific, technical sense. A **random sampling** procedure is one in which all subjects have an equal chance of being selected. In this case, random does not mean haphazard or arbitrary as it frequently does in ordinary conversation. In **non-random sampling**, subjects are not selected by chance. Non-random sampling is also called haphazard sampling. Examples include contacting shoppers at a shopping center, or calling up the first 100 people on a phone list. Non-random sampling does not allow the survey designer to generalize beyond the people being interviewed.

A sampling procedure is never good or bad in itself; it must be evaluated by its ability to satisfy the objectives of the survey, given the amount of time and money available. Although random sampling is preferred in every case, time and respondent availability sometimes make it very difficult.

77

Two of the most frequently used random sampling methods are simple random sampling and cluster sampling. If you have a complete list of everyone in a target population and have equal access to those persons, you can use a **simple random sampling** procedure. If you don't have a complete list of everyone in your target population, you can identify a location where your target population may be and randomly select persons from that location. This is a variation on simple random sampling called **clustering**.

Simple Random Sampling Example	Cluster Sampling Example
Your target population is the student body of Lancaster High School. You have a complete list of all Lancaster High students. You randomly select every fourth student on your list until you have reached your desired sample size. Then you mail a survey to those students selected, at their homeroom addresses.	Your target population is the student body of Lancaster High School. You do not have a complete list of all Lancaster High students. You randomly select homerooms on each grade level. For each homeroom you randomly select a student until you reach your desired sample size. Then you contact the students in their homerooms.

SAMPLING BIAS

The sampling procedure may oversample or undersample certain categories of respondents. For example, a list of all the doctors in a certain region may not be completely up to date and thus will underreport younger doctors and those who have recently moved into the area. Sampling directly from the telephone book will also have some bias. It will bypass any individuals who do not own a telephone, or who have unlisted telephone numbers.

Make sure that the bias likely to be found in your sampling procedure will not seriously affect the results of your survey in any way that is critical. For example, if you feel that omitting people with unlisted telephone numbers will seriously misrepresent your target population, you may undertake any of the following steps:

- Supplement with a door-to-door survey

- Randomly dial numbers

- Acknowledge the bias in your report and specify how this bias may affect your survey results

78

EXAMPLE

EXERCISE 5.2: CHOOSING A SAMPLE

(A) INDICATE THE TOTAL SIZE OF THE SAMPLE AND THE APPROXIMATE PERCENTAGE THIS REPRESENTS OF THE TARGET POPULATION:

A sample of 200 students will be selected, approximately 10% of the target population.

(B) INDICATE WHICH PROCEDURES YOU WILL USE TO SELECT THE SAMPLE. BE SPECIFIC AS TO THE PROCEDURE YOU WILL FOLLOW TO SELECT THE NAMES OF THE PEOPLE TO BE CONTACTED:

A list will be obtained from the Riverdale High School's attendance office of all the students currently enrolled in grades nine through twelve. Since a complete and current list of students in each homeroom is available, random sampling will be used. The random sampling form of clustering will ensure a distribution of students in each grade proportionate to that of the target population. Random sampling will be used to select five students from each of the forty homerooms. From each homeroom list, every fifth student, up to a total of five, will be selected.

(C) IDENTIFY ONE OR MORE MAJOR SOURCES OF SAMPLING BIAS AND WHAT REMEDIES YOU WILL USE:

The list of students in each homeroom does not include those students who have dropped out of school. As these teenagers may be greatly in need of suicide prevention workshops, we will try to locate them by examining past attendance lists.

79

STEP 5.3
DECIDING ON A METHOD OF CONTACT

Once the population and the sampling procedure have been determined, decide on how the respondents will be contacted. Three methods are possible—face-to-face interviews, telephone interviews, and mail questionnaires. Each method has different strengths and limitations.

RESPONSE RATE

One of the main differences among the three methods of contact is the different response rate which can be obtained from each. Face-to-face contact normally yields the largest fraction of completed surveys, telephone contact the second largest, and mail contact the least. The usual ranges of response rates for the three types of contact are shown below:

Expected Ranges of Response Rates	
Face-to-face	75 - 90% response rate
Telephone	40 -75% response rate
Mail	5 - 50% response rate

No matter which method of contact you use, you can do some things to increase the response rate:

- Keep the questionnaire short
- Make items easy to answer
- Use closed-choice questions
- Get the respondents interested in the topic
- Avoid embarrassing questions as much as possible

The three methods of contact differ in other important respects besides response rate. Each of the three has particular advantages and disadvantages that you should consider in deciding which method of contact to use in your planned survey.

80

ADVANTAGES AND DISADVANTAGES OF THREE METHODS OF CONTACTING SURVEY RESPONDENTS

	FACE-TO-FACE	TELEPHONE	MAIL
ADVANTAGES	Chance to stimulate subject's interest	Same as face-to-face	Low cost
	Supportive responses by interviewer, producing better answers	Same as face-to-face	Respondent can decide when and where to complete it
	Chance to do follow-up questions, clear up unclear answers, answer questions in the mind of respondent	Same as face-to-face	Respondent may feel more comfortable answering personal questions in private
	Responses independent of literacy or physical disabilities of respondent	Same as face-to-face	Respondent may be less threatened by mail rather than direct contact
DISADVANTAGES	Very expensive; requires much time	Somewhat demanding of time	Respondent must take initiative to return the questionnaire
	Dependent on skill of interviewer	Same as face-to-face	Questionnaire may be dismissed as "junk mail" unless sent first class and accompanied by personal cover letter
	Respondent may be more reluctant to answer personal questions	Respondent may easily terminate survey by hanging up	Respondent may ignore some questions

EXAMPLE

EXERCISE 5.3: DECIDING ON A METHOD OF CONTACT

(A)   INDICATE WHICH OF THE THREE METHODS OF CONTACT YOU WOULD USE:

    Intra-school mail

(B)   JUSTIFY YOUR SELECTION:

    A questionnaire distributed to students in their homerooms through
    the school's mail system would be the most efficient way to obtain
    information from the teenagers. There would be no cost for postage and
    the students can be reached any morning in their homerooms.

(C)   ESTIMATE A RESPONSE RATE AND HOW MANY PEOPLE YOU EXPECT TO CONTACT
      TO ACHIEVE YOUR DESIRED SAMPLE SIZE. INDICATE THE REASONS FOR YOUR
      ESTIMATED RESPONSE RATE:

    Assumed Response Rate: 50%

    The topic is one of interest to high school students and the ques-
    tionnaire is short. Therefore, I will send out 400 questionnaires, in
    order to achieve a sample of 200.

STEP 5.4
CREATING THE QUESTIONS

After determining the method of gathering information, the researcher must decide if the survey will contain questions that are closed-choice questions, open-ended questions, or some combination of the two.

CLOSED-CHOICE QUESTIONS

This type of question limits the kinds of answers the subject gives, requiring a choice of one or more of the answers provided by the questionnaire.

An example of a closed-choice question is as follows:

There has been a great deal of concern about the rising cost of food. How do you handle the problem of rising food costs? (Check all that apply.)

_____ purchase cheaper types of food
_____ substitute other types of food in your daily diet
_____ purchase large amounts of an item that is on sale
_____ eat at restaurants less often
_____ invite fewer people over to eat a meal at your home
_____ don't know

An example of a closed-choice scale for opinions about a proposed policy is as follows:

_____STRONGLY FAVOR ___FAVOR ___NEUTRAL ___OPPOSE ____STRONGLY OPPOSE

Still another example is this scale for obtaining information about the frequency of an activity:

_____ AT LEAST ONCE A WEEK
_____ LESS THAN ONCE A WEEK, BUT AT LEAST ONCE A MONTH
_____ LESS THAN ONCE A MONTH
_____ NEVER

The major advantage of closed-choice questions is that the answers given by the subjects are comparable and limited in number. This makes coding and analyzing the data much easier. In addition, this type of question requires less skill and effort on the part of the interviewer and is easier for the subject to answer. The most serious drawback

83

is that the closed-choice question may put words in the subjects' mouths by supplying answers they may not have thought of themselves. Most subjects do not want to admit that they have not heard of an issue, and they can conceal this fact by choosing one of the answers provided.

Closed-choice questions may introduce bias, so construct them carefully. The wording and the ordering of questions, and the limiting of the choice of answers can all influence the respondents' replies. For example, consider the question:

How much do you support clean air?

_____ Slightly _____ Moderately _____ Strongly

The question introduces bias in two ways: (1) it ignores the aspect of cost or priorities such as higher taxes or clear air vs. higher fuel and energy costs, and (2) the choices given allow only positive responses, excluding neutrality or opposition. Closed-choice questions must allow for an equal number of responses on both sides of any issue. A better question would be:

This state is presently spending $1 million a year on improving air quality. How much money do you think the government should spend?

_____Much More _____More _____Same _____Less _____Much Less

OPEN-ENDED QUESTIONS

Open-ended questions are those that allow subjects to answer the questions without restrictions imposed by the questionnaire. However, responses to open-ended questions may be extremely difficult to classify. Open-ended questions, therefore, should be used only when they are clearly appropriate. An example of an appropriate open-ended question is: "What do you think are the main causes for the rising price of food?"

The most important advantage of the open-ended question is that the respondents can answer using their own reasoning and thinking patterns. In doing so, they may suggest new ideas. Another advantage is that open-ended questions do not select answers for respondents, which may be a problem with closed-choice questions. Finally, this type of question can provide a chance for subjects to "warm up" at the beginning of the interview.

The major limitation to open-ended questions lies in the difficulty of making meaningful comparisons among respondents. Another problem is that interviewers require training to make sure that they conduct interviews properly. Finally, analyzing open-ended responses is more time-consuming than closed-choice responses. Whenever you decide to include open-ended questions, you must also include the specific procedures for coding the answers. Then you can make generalizations about the responses.

84

EXAMPLE

EXERCISE 5.4: CREATING THE QUESTIONS

PROVIDE TWO EXAMPLES OF QUESTIONS TO BE USED IN THE SURVEY, INCLUDING THE RESPONSE CATEGORIES FOR CLOSED-CHOICE QUESTIONS. IF YOU USE OPEN-ENDED QUESTIONS, INDICATE WHY AND INDICATE WHAT CATEGORIES WILL BE USED TO CODE THE ANSWERS:

QUESTION 1: How much exposure have you had to information concerning the problem of teenage suicide? Check each of the sources of any information you have received.

_____ School workshops
_____ Other workshops (indicate where) _____
_____ Pamphlets
_____ Television programs
_____ Newspaper stories
_____ Magazine articles
_____ Other (Please specify what) _____

QUESTION 2: What do you think causes most teenage suicide?

The responses will be classified into four categories:

    1) blame placed on self
    2) blame placed on environment
    3) cannot be coded
    4) no answer

I decided to use an open-ended question because the subject is very sensitive and people have many different opinions. This type of question allows the respondent to answer freely.

85

STEP 5.5
ESTIMATING THE COSTS OF A SURVEY
OR INTERVIEW

Surveys and interviews can be costly. Always weigh the costs of the research with the expected benefits that the information will provide. You should never assume that time spent in doing a survey is free. Although specifying exact costs is very difficult until you have had extensive experience in conducting surveys and interviews, at least be aware of immediate costs. The following costs should be considered:

1. Design time—how long does the survey design take to complete? Refer to Steps 5.1 – 5.4 on the preceding pages.

2. Printing costs or interview costs.

3. Transportation costs—how much does it cost to get to respondents for face-to-face interviews?

4. Communication costs—how much does the use of the telephone or mail cost?

5. Analyzing the information—how much time does it take to count the responses or to put the responses on a computer and run the computer program?

6. Report preparation costs—how much time does it take and what labor costs are involved (e.g., typing, copying) to prepare the report?

EXAMPLE

EXERCISE 5.5: ESTIMATING THE COSTS OF A SURVEY OR INTERVIEW

FOR THE SURVEY YOU HAVE BEEN DESIGNING, ESTIMATE THE COSTS USING THE CATEGORIES PROVIDED BELOW. FOR PAYMENT TO INDIVIDUALS INDICATE HOURS MULTIPLIED BY FEE PER HOUR AS A SUBCATEGORY. INDICATE THE AMOUNTS UNDER EACH SUBCATEGORY. EXPLAIN EXPENDITURES. PLACE THE TOTAL FOR EACH CATEGORY UNDER "TOTAL". (USE THE HOURLY FEE FROM THE EXAMPLE UNLESS YOU HAVE OBTAINED OTHER FIGURES):

CATEGORY AND COMMENT   TOTAL

1.   DESIGN: $500

    1.1   LABOR: 10 hours X $50 = $500

    1.2   OTHER: None

2.   PRINTING COSTS $150

    2.1   LABOR: 5 hours x $10 = $50

    2.2   OTHER: Paper and supplies, $100

3.   TRANSPORTATION COSTS $ ---

    3.1   LABOR: None since this is a mail survey.

    3.2   OTHER: None

4.   MAIL OR INTERVIEW COSTS $ ---

    4.1   LABOR: None since the survey will be distributed through the school mail system

    4.2   OTHER: None

5.   ANALYSIS COSTS $ 570

    5.1   LABOR: 20 hours x $25 = $500 for data input, computer operations, and statistical consulting.

    5.2   OTHER: $70 for travel and expenses to meet with advisers.

6.   REPORT PREPARATION $230

    6.1   LABOR: 10 hours x $8 = $80 for editor's time

    6.2   OTHER: $150 for typing and reproduction.

TOTAL $1,450

SUMMARY

CONCEPTS	DEFINITIONS	TASKS	EXAMPLES
Target Population	Group of people to which the survey applies	Identify precisely the people by location, role, and important characteristics	All individuals in N.J. above the age of 16
Sample	Portion of the population which is actually surveyed	Develop procedures for selecting from the target population the most representative sample	Simple random sample
Closed-Choice Question	Type of question in which respondent has a limited number of alternative answers	Prepare a precise and clearly stated question with a small number of distinct answers	Do you have a full-time job? Yes___ No ___
Open-Ended Question	Type of question in which respondent can answer in his or her own words	Prepare a clearly stated question and codes for expected answers	What is the reason for your unemployment? (Code whether blame is placed on government, business, education, or self.)

PARTICIPATION ACTIVITY: Providing Survey Research to Players

1. Select a policy issue that you (or your group) would be interested in studying.

2. Identify a specific player that is interested in the selected issue. Contact the player directly by phone or mail. If you are not sure how to identify and locate the player, refer to Chapter 6, which provides the necessary information. If you have trouble contacting the actual player or one of the player's assistants, you can still undertake the project and submit it without prior contact. However, it is better to get help from the player at the outset. If you are unable to arrange a meeting, skip the next step and go directly to 4.

3. Explain to the player that you would like to design and conduct a survey on an issue of interest to both of you. Provide an overview of how the survey would be designed and conducted. Indicate that you will be contacting the player in a week to determine if the player is interested in having the survey conducted.

   If there is interest, meet with the player to reach an agreement on the following items:

   - type of information to be acquired
   - description of target population
   - sampling procedures
   - methods of contact
   - questions
   - date when report will be submitted

4. Using the guidelines provided in this chapter, develop a survey design. Have your teacher approve the design and then implement the survey. Collect the information carefully, and analyze your results.

5. Complete the report on the agreed-upon date, submit it in written form, and offer to make an oral presentation.

6. Thank the player for the opportunity to provide the service. Provide a report to the class on your experience.

CHAPTER 6

GATHERING INFORMATION
FROM KNOWLEDGEABLE PEOPLE

YOUR GOAL

To identify and interview people who have specialized information on a public policy issue.

INTRODUCTION

Information about public policy issues gathered from library research and formal surveys often needs to be supplemented by information obtained from knowledgeable people, including:

- Government officials who make or administer the laws

- Individuals and pressure group members who work to influence the public policy-making process

- Professional observers such as journalists and academic researchers

Because these people have a direct stake in public policy issues, they are good sources of information.

This chapter will describe what kinds of information can be obtained from these sources, how to locate key people to interview, and how to get the most detailed and accurate information possible.

STEP 6.1
PREPARING FOR THE INTERVIEW

Knowledgeable people can provide:

- Suggestions on material you might find in the library or derive from surveys. The expert may even have copies of studies for you to examine
- Details of existing laws, administrative procedures, judicial decisions, and other information about activities leading to the making of public policies

Knowledgeable people are more likely to help you if they are convinced that you are interested in the subject. For that reason, before directly contacting a knowledgeable individual, you must have a basic knowledge of the subject and a clear idea of the information you want to obtain.

In deciding what specific information you want to obtain, consider the following example. Suppose that you are interested in your school district's policy on closing school for bad weather. Here are some questions to ask: Who makes the final decision? Are there guidelines from the state about the factors that should be considered? How does the person making the decision get information about the weather conditions?

Develop a checklist using the categories discussed in Chapter 1. Think of questions you might ask with respect to the following:

1. Public policy—What relevant laws exist or are proposed? Which administrative agencies are responsible for implementing the laws? Have there been relevant judicial decisions?

2. Social conditions—What are they? What studies exist on them? What studies are planned? How different will they be in the future?

3. Players—Who are the key individuals, groups, and institutions responsible for the policy? Are they for or against the policy? How much power do they have? How important is the issue to them?

EXAMPLE

EXERCISE 6.1: PREPARING FOR THE INTERVIEW

(A) DESCRIBE A PUBLIC POLICY TOPIC ABOUT WHICH YOU WANT TO OBTAIN INFORMATION:

Homeless people in Syracuse, New York

(B) LIST THREE QUESTIONS ABOUT THE PUBLIC POLICY:

1. What is the police department's policy about arresting people sleeping on the streets?

2. What have past policies been on constructing emergency shelters?

3. To what extent does deinstitutionalization of psychiatric patients contribute to the number of homeless people?

(C) LIST THREE QUESTIONS ABOUT SOCIAL CONDITIONS:

1. How many people are homeless in Syracuse?

2. How many emergency shelters exist in the city?

3. How many homeless people have been hospitalized for exposure or mugging?

(D) LIST THREE QUESTIONS ABOUT PLAYERS:

1. How important is the issue of homelessness to the mayor?

2. Does the city council favor allocating funds to construct more emergency shelters?

3. Which groups lobby government officials in favor of aiding homeless people?

STEP 6.2
LOCATING KNOWLEDGEABLE
PEOPLE TO INTERVIEW

Once you have some basic background information about your public policy, and you have thought of questions you might ask, you should be able to select the people you might want to contact for more information. For example, your investigation of school policy on the cancellation of classes for bad weather would take you to the district office. You might want to contact the superintendent or an assistant superintendent. You may also want to talk to one of your teachers and an officer of the parent-teacher organization.

In deciding on which knowledgeable people you wish to contact, you need to balance how easy it would be to contact the person with how much information the person is likely to have. Generally, the people with the best information are the most difficult to contact. You may want to begin with someone that you can get in touch with easily and ask for suggestions and even an introduction to someone more knowledgeable.

From your background research, select the names of people and organizations that are mentioned in the news, books, and articles. You may also try to contact journalists and academic researchers who have published articles or books on the subject.

The telephone book is an essential tool for locating knowledgeable people, even if you do not have a specific name of an individual or organization. Phone numbers of local, state, and federal government offices appear in the phone book in a separate section called the **blue pages**. Non-government agencies are listed in the **yellow pages** under such headings as "social service organizations," "environmental conservation and ecological organizations," "drug abuse and addiction information and treatment," and "business and trade organizations." Formal pressure groups may be listed in the yellow pages by subject or in the general (white pages) section by name.

If you have located the organization in the phone book but do not know the name of a specific individual who can answer your questions, take the following steps: (1) call the main number, (2) identify youself, (3) state the purpose of your call, and (4) ask for the name of someone who can provide the information on your topic.

EXAMPLE

EXERCISE 6.2: LOCATING
KNOWLEDGEABLE PEOPLE TO INTERVIEW

USING THE PUBLIC POLICY TOPIC DESCRIBED IN EXERCISE 6.1, LIST THE NAME, ORGANI-
ZATION, COMPLETE MAILING ADDRESS, AND TELEPHONE NUMBER OF TWO INDIVIDUALS
WHO CAN PROVIDE INFORMATION ON THE TOPIC. BELOW THE LISTING, BRIEFLY DE-
SCRIBE HOW YOU IDENTIFIED AND LOCATED EACH PERSON:

NAME AND POSITION: Clarence Jordan, Director
ORGANIZATION: Rescue Mission Alliance
ADDRESS: 120 Gifford Street, Syracuse, New York 13202
TELEPHONE: 472-6251

DESCRIPTION OF HOW OBTAINED:

The Rescue Mission Alliance is listed in the yellow pages of the phonebook
under the heading "Social Service Organizations." Mr. Jordan's name was
obtained from the person who answered the main telephone number.

NAME AND POSITION: Robert Stone, Director
ORGANIZATION: Onondaga County Department of Social Services
ADDRESS: 421 Montgomery Street, Syracuse, New York 13202
TELEPHONE: 425-2792

DESCRIPTION OF HOW OBTAINED:

Robert Stone was interviewed on the 6 o'clock television news. His phone
number was obtained from the government listings in the phone book.

STEP 6.3
OBTAINING DETAILED AND
ACCURATE INFORMATION

Once you have decided on the people and organizations you wish to contact, decide whether you will use the phone, make a personal visit, or write a letter. Initially, phone to make sure that the person is willing and able to provide the information. Obtaining the information at the time of the initial phone call would be most efficient. However, the interviewee may prefer a written request or a personal visit. The written request may be part of the organization's procedure. A personal visit, if possible, is always useful because you may be introduced to other people to interview and you may be able to study or even acquire written material. Always ask the people you interview to suggest others to be contacted. In addition, ask for written material from the individual or agency that may provide information.

Obtaining detailed and accurate information from a knowledgeable person requires you to be as informed as possible. We have already emphasized that you should have background information on the public policy issues in order to select the people you want to contact in the first place. Once you contact that person, the more specific the questions, the better.

Various types of people may give you biased information. Government officials will almost always provide you with the official viewpoint and will try to avoid controversy. As a result, the information will tend to be carefully worded and may be vague. People who are trying to influence government policy will explain things in ways that support their positions and self-interest. Journalists and academic researchers will claim they are objective, but they may also have a particular orientation. Also, the person you are talking to may not have the information and may guess at it.

The best way to guard against possible bias is to ask the same question of two or more people that you know have different views on the public policy issue. If people on different sides of an issue give you the same information, you can have some confidence that the information is accurate. If you receive conflicting information, you may have to interview additional people, check other sources, or at least realize the questionable nature of the information.

EXAMPLE

EXERCISE 6.3: OBTAINING
DETAILED AND ACCURATE INFORMATION

(A)   LIST THREE SPECIFIC QUESTIONS THAT YOU WOULD ASK ONE OF THE PEOPLE
      IDENTIFIED IN EXERCISE 6.2:

EXPERT   QUESTIONS

Robert Stone, Director   1. How many homeless people live in
Onondaga County   the city?
Department of Social
Services   2. Does the police department arrest people
                                   sleeping on the streets?

                                3. What services does your organization
                                   provide for homeless people?

(B)   DISCUSS HOW YOU WOULD CHECK FOR ACCURACY ON ONE OF THE THREE
      QUESTIONS ASKED ABOVE:

  I would put question 1 to a different government agency, such as the
mayor's office, along with one or two private agencies. If their estimates were different, I would use the average of all the estimates.

97

SUMMARY

TERMS	DEFINITIONS	SKILLS	EXAMPLES
Knowledgeable People	People who have specialized information on a public policy issue	Identify people that can supply information and references on your topic	Clarence Jordan, Director, Rescue Mission Alliance Robert Stone, Director, Onondaga County Department of Social Services
Yellow Pages	Section of the telephone book that provides listings of businesses and organizations by subject heading	Locate the names of businesses and organizations related to your public policy issue using subject headings	Social Service Organizations Business and Trade Organizations
Blue Pages	Section of the telephone book that lists all government offices (federal, state, county, local) in the area	Identify the office that can best supply information on a given issue	Onondaga County Department of Social Services

PART III: NUMBERS AND GRAPHS

This section introduces you to the basic methods of data presentation and analysis that can be used in the study of public policy issues. The section is written with the assumption that you have had little or no experience in data presentation.

Chapter 7: Using Numbers and Graphs

Step 1: Scaling Numbers

Step 2: Presenting Data with Tables

Step 3: Comparing with Bar Graphs

Step 4: Using Trend Lines

Step 5: Displaying Components with Pie Charts

Step 6: Describing Differences with Percentages

Step 7: Using Scatterplots and Pearson's r

CHAPTER 7

USING NUMBERS AND GRAPHS

YOUR GOAL

To interpret conditions relevant to public policy using numbers and graphs.

INTRODUCTION

The making and analyzing of policy are increasingly dependent on the use of numbers and graphs. We use numbers in almost every aspect of communication. Our favorite sports team is described as "Number 1." Your academic performance is described by the numerical grades you receive. The use of numbers and graphs to examine conditions is usually called **statistical analysis**.

Numbers and graphs should be presented in a form that is both interesting and clear. In this chapter, you will work through several examples of how to present data. Once you learn the basics, you will find that with numbers and graphs, you can present many ideas more concisely than with words.

People collect and interpret numerical data when they analyze public policy issues for two primary reasons:

1. Numbers help us to acquire a general grasp of factors affecting public policy issues.

2. Numbers give us a precise statement about those factors. Then, comparisons can be made between different locations, periods of time, and target populations.

Bad Example:	More people are unemployed this year than last year.	Good Example:	Unemployment in the United States is 9.6% this year, compared to 8.4% last year.

The second statement is preferable because it gives us both a general picture of social conditions and a precise measure. We see that unemployment is worse this year than last and by how much.

Numbers and graphs can be used in all areas of public policy analysis, but they are most extensively used to measure social conditions. Figure 7.1 presents examples of data that might be found in each of the three components of public policy issues described in Chapter 1.

Figure 7.1: Examples of Numerical Data Used to Describe the Components of Public Policy Issues

SOCIAL CONDITIONS

- Unemployment
- Inflation
- Economic growth
- Traffic fatalities
- Drug use
- School attendance

PLAYERS

- Survey of attitudes of legislators
- Political contributions received
- Legislative voting records

PUBLIC POLICIES

- Government expenditures
- Tax rates
- Tax revenues
- Minimum wage

The use of numbers and graphs in public policy analysis requires that you have completed three essential tasks:

1. Select the most appropriate numerical information available. Such information is difficult to obtain in most cases. Use skills developed in Chapter 4 to locate the information.

2. Select the most appropriate type of analysis and display. This chapter will review the most frequently used types of analysis and display and indicate their appropriate use.

3. Make an interpretation that relates the analysis and display to the public policy. The guidelines to providing good interpretations follow.

INTERPRETING NUMERICAL DATA

Interpreting numerical information means explaining the reasons behind the information and drawing an inference about what the information means. More specifically, interpretation is performing the following types of analysis (as discussed in Chapter 3) with numerical information:

1. *Summarizing* what the numbers say (part of monitoring)

2. *Explaining* why the numbers are the way they are

3. *Forecasting* what the numbers might look like in the future

4. *Evaluating* the numbers in relation to a clear set of policy goals

5. *Prescribing* a public policy based on the numbers and conclusions drawn from the explanation, forecast, and evaluation

Assuming the information and statistics are done correctly, a good interpretation includes:

1. A brief summary of the main point or points of the display or statistical analysis

2. An explanation of at least one of the major underlying factors contributing to the main point

3. At least one forecast, evaluation, or prescription

A particular display may generate many different, even conflicting, interpretations. Consider the trend line in Figure 7.2, and the interpretation that follows it. The interpretation includes a brief summary of one main point, one possible explanation, and an example of a forecast, an evaluation, and a prescription. Different forecasts, evaluations, and prescriptions may be based on the same graph. You could probably develop different interpretations yourself.

Figure 7.2: Percentage of Women in the United States Military Services, 1971 – 1987

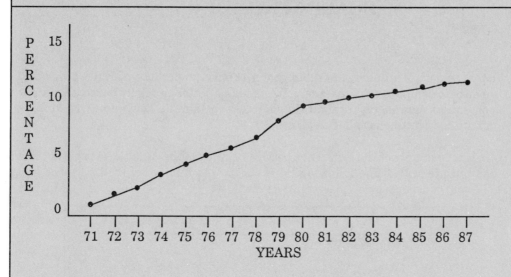

Department of Defense Report, Published in *USA Today*, October 27, 1987, p. 5A.

The *main point* of the figure is that the percentage of women in the armed forces has substantially increased during the 1970s and 1980s. During the past ten years the percentage has almost doubled. One *explanation* of this is that the military's increased effort to recruit females has been effective. We can *forecast* that the percentage will continue to increase. However, the increase has been slowing in recent years, and will probably continue growing at a slower rate, to about 15% over the next ten years. The reason for forecasting that the growth will continue to be slow is that many American women still reject the military as a career. Well-publicized incidents of discrimination against women in the military will also slow the increase of women in the military. An *evaluation* of this situation is that equality between the sexes does not exist in the armed forces. A *prescription* is that the military should increase its efforts at recruiting females, and should work hard to eliminate discrimination against females who are in the service.

103

STEP 7.1
SCALING NUMBERS

Whenever you use numbers in a table, graph, or chart, report them in such a way that they are easy to compare and interpret. It is usually better to report percentages, per capita, or similar figures, rather than simple totals and similar raw numbers. Making the numbers comparable is called **scaling**.

Here is an example of the difference between raw numbers and those reported in a more appropriate scale. The following table shows the number of traffic deaths in a selected group of states:

Figure 7.3:	Total Traffic Deaths in Selected States, 1985
State	Deaths
California	4,999
New York	2,065
Alabama	939
Massachusetts	663
New Mexico	497

Source: National Safety Council, reported in *The World Almanac and Book of Facts*. New York: Newspaper Enterprise Association, 1986. p. 781.

Does this mean that California and New York are the most dangerous places to drive, and that Alabama, Massachusetts, and New Mexico are the safest? Not necessarily. Part of the reason that California and New York have so many traffic deaths, and that Alabama, Massachusetts and New Mexico have so few deaths may be the difference in the number of miles driven in each state. It is better to report the traffic death rate, that is, the number of deaths divided by the number of miles driven in each state. The usual automobile traffic death rate is the number of deaths for each 100 million miles driven. Since California and New York have very large numbers of miles driven, their high traffic death totals are divided by large numbers, which tends to lower their death rate. On the other hand, Alabama and New Mexico have fewer drivers and fewer roads, so their traffic death totals are divided by a smaller number, making their death rate higher. What about Massachusetts? It has a fairly low death total; it also has a fairly large population and number of miles driven. Where will it rank when its traffic death total is divided by the miles driven in the state?

The answer is given in the following table, where the states are listed according to their traffic death rate–total traffic deaths per 100 million miles driven:

Figure 7.4:   Traffic Death Rate per 100 Million Miles Driven, Selected States, 1985

State	Deaths per 100 Million Miles Driven
New Mexico	4.3
Alabama	3.1
California	2.9
New York	2.4
Massachusetts	1.7

Source: National Safety Council reported in *The World Almanac and Book of Facts,* New York: Newspaper Enterprise Association, 1986. p. 781.

Here the rank is quite different. New Mexico and Alabama have the highest death rates, California and New York are in the middle, and Massachusetts has the lowest traffic death rate.

The scale you use for reporting numbers depends on the kind of information you are reporting. Often percentages are used, which means that each number is divided by the same total. This shows what fraction each number represents of the entire total. Examples of such presentations include budget figures, racial composition of a city, and the number of males and females in particular occupational groups. Another common way of presenting numbers is on a per capita basis, in which each number is divided by the population of the unit (for example, school, city, or state) being reported. Examples include crime rates in different neighborhoods of a city, and income levels in different cities. Sometimes, if numbers involved are quite small, the figure is reported not in terms of the number of people, but in terms of 100 or 1000 people. Some commonly used figures, such as unemployment rates, are reported as percentages—which means the number of unemployed individuals for each 100 people looking for work.

To convert raw numbers to numbers that can be easily compared, you need to complete the following steps:

1. Decide if the raw number is adequate without making some conversion. This is possible in some rare instances. If not, go to step 2.

For the example on traffic deaths, the raw numbers for traffic deaths are:

California: 4999   Alabama: 939
New York: 2065   New Mexico: 497
Massachusetts: 663

105

2. Choose the unit that should be divided into the raw number to allow for comparisons. As noted above, you may want to use the total which would give you a percentage or per capita figure.

For the example on traffic deaths the unit chosen is 100 million miles travelled:

California - 1724   Alabama - 303
New York - 860   New Mexico - 116
Massachusetts - 390

3. Divide the raw number by the unit number. Clearly label the number and provide a specific description of the source.

For the example on traffic deaths, the division and scaled numbers (total traffic deaths per 100 million miles travelled) are:

California $\dfrac{4999}{1724} = 2.9$ Alabama $\dfrac{939}{303} = 3.1$

New York $\dfrac{2065}{860} = 2.4$ New Mexico $\dfrac{497}{116} = 4.3$

Massachusetts $\dfrac{663}{390} = 1.7$

Source: National Safety Council reported in *The World Almanac and Book of Facts*. New York: Newspaper Enterprise Association, 1986. p. 781.

EXAMPLE

EXERCISE 7.1: SCALING NUMBERS

(A) IDENTIFY AT LEAST TWO NUMBERS THAT INDICATE SOMETHING ABOUT PLAYERS, POLICIES, OR SOCIAL CONDITIONS. INDICATE THE GEOGRAPHICAL LEVEL, THE TIME PERIOD, AND THE PRECISE DESCRIPTION OF THE NUMBERS:

Transportation accident deaths in the United States for 1984 were 49 for buses, 4 for trains, and 17 for airlines.

(B) PRESENT THE NUMBERS USED TO SCALE THE RAW NUMBERS WITH A PRECISE DESCRIPTION OF THE NUMBER:

Total miles traveled were 90 billion for buses, 11.1 billion for trains, and 231.7 billion for airlines.

(C) PRESENT AND LABEL THE RESULTING SCALED NUMBERS:

Deaths per billion miles travelled
Buses =.544   Trains =.363   Commercial airlines =.073

(D) THE SOURCE OF YOUR FIGURES:

National Safety Council, reported in The World Almanac and Book of Facts. New York: Newspaper Enterprise Association, 1986. p.780.

(E) BRIEFLY COMPARE DIFFERENCES BETWEEN RAW AND SCALED FIGURES:

Bus travel has the highest raw total deaths, and also the highest rate when divided by billions of miles traveled. Although airlines have more deaths than trains, on a per mileage rate, airlines have many fewer deaths than trains.

STEP 7.2
PRESENTING DATA WITH TABLES

Data must be presented in a form that is both interesting and clear. Stringing numbers together in a text does not accomplish either of these goals. For example, consider the following hypothetical example:

A recent study, "Committee for the Aging: Research and Education" (CARE) indicates that, in 1920, the percentage of the United States population 60 years of age and over was 6%; in 1940, the percentage was 8%; in 1960, it was 13%; in 1980, it was 15%; and in 2000, it is forecast to be 20%.

Such information is difficult to understand presented in this way. If arranged in a table, as below, it is much easier to read.

Figure 7.5: Percentage of the United States Population at Least 60 Years of Age, 1920 – 2000

YEAR	PERCENTAGE
1920	6%
1940	8%
1960	13%
1980	15%
2000(forecast)	20%

Source: "Committee for the Aging: Research and Education," New York: CARE, 1985.

Tables are a widely used and accepted means of organizing small sets of data for rapid visualization and understanding. A table requires:

- A title which clearly explains its nature

- Data elements carefully listed under headings which clearly specify units of measure

- Documentation of the data source. Indicate the title of the source and a complete bibliographical reference, as described in Chapter 4. Just listing the organization issuing the information is not adequate. If the source is a newspaper, cite the title of the story, date, and page number.

EXAMPLE

EXERCISE 7.2: PRESENTING DATA WITH TABLES

(A) CONSTRUCT A TABLE RELEVANT TO A PUBLIC POLICY ISSUE. PROVIDE THE SOURCE OF THE DATA:

U.S. BICYCLE DEATHS, 1955-1985

YEAR	MILLIONS OF CYCLES	DEATHS	DEATHS PER 100,000 CYCLES
1955	7.8	750	9.59
1960	13.8	440	3.18
1965	28.2	460	1.63
1970	56.5	780	1.38
1975	100.0	1200	1.20
1980	105.5	1100	1.04
1985	106.1	1000	0.94

Source: National Safety Council, reported in The World Almanac and Book of Facts. New York: Newspaper Enterprise Association, 1986. p.781.

(B) WRITE AN INTERPRETATION BELOW. CONTINUE ON ANOTHER PAGE IF NECESSARY. BRIEFLY SUMMARIZE A MAJOR POINT PORTRAYED AND PROVIDE AN EXPLANATION. IN ADDITION, PROVIDE AN EXAMPLE OF ONE OF THE FOLLOWING: A FORECAST, AN EVALUATION, OR A PRESCRIPTION RELATED TO WHAT IS PORTRAYED. CLEARLY LABEL EACH TYPE OF ANALYSIS THAT YOU PROVIDE:

The main point is that although the number of deaths has generally increased, the deaths per cycle has declined. One reason is that with the increase in the number of cycles over time, more attention has been paid to safety on the part of both cyclists and automobile drivers. The forecast is that although the rate has been declining to around 1.00 per 100,000 bicycles, the trend is unlikely to drop any further. Since some people are always going to be careless, and since young people are learning to ride bicycles each year, some fatal accidents will always occur.

109

STEP 7.3
COMPARING WITH BAR GRAPHS

An even more striking way of presenting data is to use a **bar graph**, which is a series of parallel bars (or similar markings) placed either vertically or horizontally to indicate totals or percentages. In the construction of a bar graph, the length of the bars and the space between them should be consistent and allow for clear visual inspection. Normally a vertical (or y) axis is drawn with the scale placed alongside, while the horizontal (or x) axis is labeled with what units are being compared or measured. Bar graphs should be used any time you want to compare two or more units (examples: states, countries, years, segments of the population).

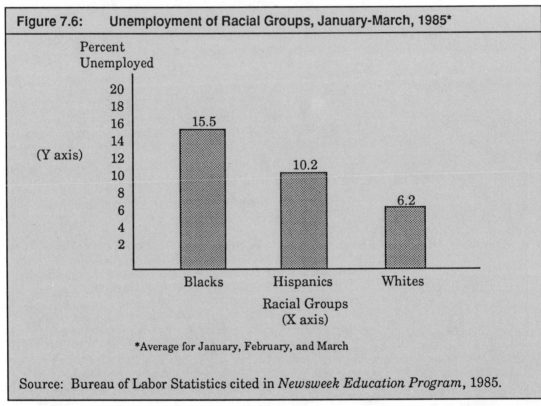

Figure 7.6: Unemployment of Racial Groups, January-March, 1985*

Percent Unemployed

(Y axis)

Racial Groups (X axis)

*Average for January, February, and March

Source: Bureau of Labor Statistics cited in *Newsweek Education Program*, 1985.

Figure 7.6 provides information on the rate of unemployment among different segments of the American population for the first quarter of 1985. Each bar represents a different segment of the American employable population, with the actual rate appearing at the top of the bar. The height of the bars allows the reader to see the difference in unemployment of different racial groups.

EXAMPLE

EXERCISE 7.3: COMPARING WITH BAR GRAPHS

(A) CONSTRUCT A BAR GRAPH RELEVANT TO A PUBLIC POLICY ISSUE. YOUR GRAPH MUST HAVE AT LEAST TWO BARS. PROVIDE THE SOURCE OF THE DATA:

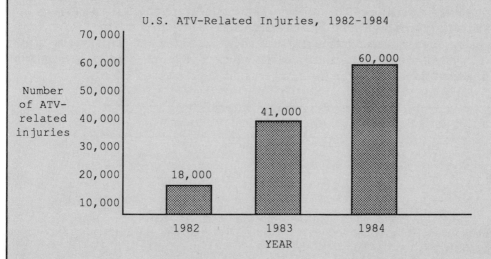

U.S. ATV-Related Injuries, 1982-1984

SOURCE: <u>Deaths from ATV Vehicles</u>. Washington, D.C.: National Safety Council, 1985.

(B) WRITE AN INTERPRETATION BELOW. CONTINUE ON ANOTHER PAGE IF NECESSARY. BRIEFLY SUMMARIZE A MAJOR POINT PORTRAYED AND PROVIDE AN EXPLANATION. IN ADDITION, PROVIDE AN EXAMPLE OF ONE OF THE FOLLOWING: A FORECAST, AN EVALUATION, OR A PRESCRIPTION RELATED TO WHAT IS PORTRAYED. CLEARLY LABEL EACH TYPE OF ANALYSIS THAT YOU PROVIDE:

The <u>main point</u> is that there has been an increase in the number of injuries on three-wheel ATV vehicles during the past two years. This increase can be <u>explained</u> in part by the growing popularity of these vehicles and a lack of government regulations. In order to reduce the very high injury rate, we <u>prescribe</u> laws comparable to those which exist for cars, motorcycles, and mopeds to regulate the use of ATVs.

111

STEP 7.4
USING TREND LINES

A **trend line** is a common form of graph. The trend line is derived from plotting time in years, months, or days on the x-axis (horizontal), and plotting the factor which is changing over time on the y-axis (vertical). This type of graph shows the progress of that which is on the y-axis over time. The trend can also be projected into the future. In the figure below, the forecasted data is represented by the dotted line. This type of display is useful in monitoring and forecasting social conditions. Figure 7.7 shows the trend from 1981 projected through 1991 on the number of deaths expected from AIDS.

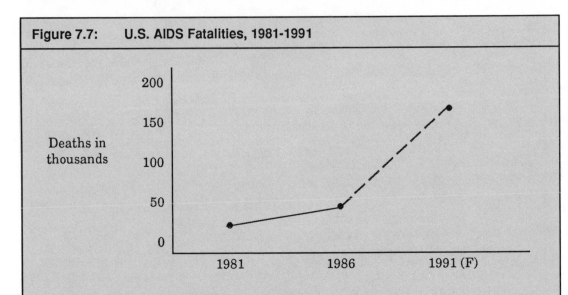

Figure 7.7: U.S. AIDS Fatalities, 1981-1991

Source: U.S. Public Health Service, Center for Disease Control, 1986. Reported in *Newsweek*, June 23, 1986, p. 68.

112

EXAMPLE

EXERCISE 7.4: USING TREND LINES

(A) CONSTRUCT A TREND LINE GRAPH RELEVANT TO A PUBLIC POLICY ISSUE. YOUR GRAPH MUST HAVE AT LEAST FIVE DATA POINTS. PROVIDE THE SOURCE OF THE DATA:

Number of Problem Banks in the United States, 1981-1985

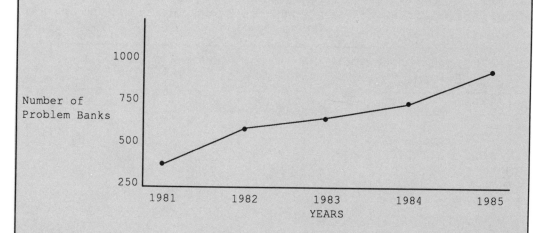

SOURCE: Regulation Activities: 1981-1985., Washington, D.C.: Federal Reserve Board, 1985.

(B) WRITE AN INTERPRETATION BELOW. CONTINUE ON ANOTHER PAGE IF NECESSARY. BRIEFLY SUMMARIZE A MAJOR POINT PORTRAYED AND PROVIDE AN EXPLANATION. IN ADDITION, PROVIDE AN EXAMPLE OF ONE OF THE FOLLOWING: A FORECAST, AN EVALUATION, OR A PRESCRIPTION RELATED TO WHAT IS PORTRAYED. CLEARLY LABEL EACH TYPE OF ANALYSIS THAT YOU PROVIDE:

The main point of the graph is that the number of banks which are viewed as "problem banks," i.e., those that could be in financial trouble, has grown substantially over the last 5 years. One explanation of this is that many of these banks are small, and they have been hit hard by the high rate of foreclosure and delinquency on loans. Prescription: The FDIC and the Federal Reserve Board must continue to assist these banks in order to prevent their failure.

113

STEP 7.5
DISPLAYING COMPONENTS WITH PIE CHARTS

A **pie chart** can be used to show how the component parts of a total are divided. The distribution of government spending or the ethnic composition of a political party are examples of subjects that can be displayed using this technique. To construct a pie chart, remember that the total of 100% is described by a circle of 360°. Thus, each percentage point is equal to an arc of 3.6°. To illustrate, we will construct a pie chart to show the distribution of people over 60 years of age as outlined in Figure 7.8. Each percent figure in Figure 7.8 is multiplied by 3.6° to determine the size of the arc that must be drawn for each segment of the pie.

Figure 7.8: Age Distribution of U.S. Population 60 and Over, Percentages Converted to Arcs

AGE GROUP	PERCENT				ARC
60 - 64 years	29.7	x	3.6	=	106.92°
65 - 74	43.6	x	3.6	=	156.96°
75 - 84	21.1	x	3.6	=	75.96°
85 and older	5.6	x	3.6	=	20.16°
	100%				360°

A protractor should be used to measure the necessary angles on the circle. The labels can go either inside or outside the circle. (Place the labels outside if the sections are especially narrow.) As illustrated in Figure 7.9, the pie chart can be a very effective technique for the visual display of data. However, some caution should be observed. Pie charts containing more than eight segments, or containing several segments with very small arcs (less than 5%), are difficult to label and interpret.

Figure 7.9: Distribution of the United States Population Age 60 and Over For 1984

Source: "Committee for the Aging: Research and Education," New York: CARE, 1985.

114

EXAMPLE

EXERCISE 7.5: DISPLAYING COMPONENTS WITH PIE CHARTS

(A) CONSTRUCT A PIE CHART WITH AT LEAST TWO PARTS AND PERCENTAGES EQUAL TO 100%. PROVIDE THE SOURCE OF THE DATA:

Sources of Health Insurance Coverage in the U.S., 1983

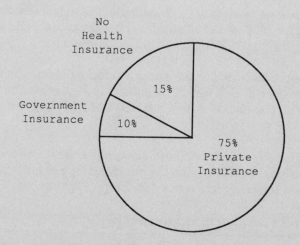

SOURCE: Robert Pear, "15% of Americans Found to Lack Health Coverage." New York Times, February 18, 1985, p. A12.

(B) WRITE AN INTERPRETATION BELOW. CONTINUE ON ANOTHER PAGE IF NECESSARY. BRIEFLY SUMMARIZE A MAJOR POINT PORTRAYED AND PROVIDE AN EXPLANATION. IN ADDITION, PROVIDE AN EXAMPLE OF ONE OF THE FOLLOWING: A FORECAST, AN EVALUATION, OR A PRESCRIPTION RELATED TO WHAT IS PORTRAYED. CLEARLY LABEL EACH TYPE OF ANALYSIS THAT YOU PROVIDE:

The main point is that 15% of Americans are not covered by health insurance. One explanation is that private insurance companies have not filled the gap left by limited government insurance programs because those left out cannot afford private insurance. An evaluation is that even 15% of the population without insurance is unacceptable in a country as wealthy as the United States.

115

STEP 7.6
DESCRIBING DIFFERENCES WITH PERCENTAGES

Percentages can be powerful tools in assessing differences between two sets of numbers. You may want to determine the differences between estimated and actual budget figures, or between one year's crime rate and another's. Percentages are used to determine precise differences in three ways:

1. *Comparison of estimated to actual* For example, the original estimate of the Federal budget deficit for 1983 was $113.65 billion, but the actual deficit was $195.4 billion. The actual figure was 73% higher than the estimate.

2. *Comparison between numbers for the same period of time* For example, in 1986, the population of the U.S.S.R. was 279.5 million and the population of the U.S. was 241.6 million. The population in the U.S.S.R. is 15.7% larger than the U.S. population.

3. *Comparison between two periods of time* For example, the number of felonies in New York City was 637,451 in 1981, while the number dropped to 538,051 in 1984. The difference between the two years was a 16% drop.

Here is the procedure for calculating percentage differences:

$$\frac{\text{New Figure} - \text{Original Figure}}{\text{Original Figure}} \times 100 = \text{Percent Difference}$$

For the example cited in point 3 above

$$\frac{\text{Total felonies (1984)} - \text{Total felonies (1981)}}{\text{Total felonies (1981)}} \times 100 = \text{Percent Difference}$$

$$\frac{538,051 - 637,451}{637,451} = \frac{-99,400}{637,451} = -.1559 = -16\%$$

If you are comparing two numbers in the same time period, you may use either one as the "new figure," and the other as the "original figure."

EXAMPLE

EXERCISE 7.6: DESCRIBING DIFFERENCES
WITH PERCENTAGES

(A) PRESENT A CALCULATION FOR A PERCENTAGE DIFFERENCE. IDENTIFY AND DOCU-
MENT THE DATA USED:

The number of people living in poverty in 1973 was 23 million
and in 1983 was 35.3 million according to "Study Absolves Reagan in
Poverty Increase," USA Today, June 11, 1985, p. 10.

$$\frac{35.3 - 23}{23} \times 100 = 53\%$$

(B) WRITE AN INTERPRETATION OF THE PERCENTAGE DIFFERENCES BELOW. BRIEFLY
SUMMARIZE A MAJOR POINT PORTRAYED AND PROVIDE AN EXPLANATION. IN
ADDITION, PROVIDE AN EXAMPLE OF ONE OF THE FOLLOWING: A FORECAST, AN
EVALUATION, OR A PRESCRIPTION RELATED TO WHAT IS PORTRAYED. CLEARLY
LABEL EACH TYPE OF ANALYSIS THAT YOU PROVIDE:

A main point is that the number of people living in poverty has increased by more than 50% over the past 10 years. A major downturn in
the economy between 1978 and 1983 is one explanation for the increase.
We forecast that poverty will not grow as much between 1983 and 1993,
since the economy performed well during the first five years of the
period.

117

STEP 7.7
USING SCATTERPLOTS AND PEARSON 'S r

A scatterplot, or scatter diagram, is a graph in which one variable is scaled along the Y (or vertical) axis and the other is scaled along the X (or horizontal) axis. Pairs of values can then be represented as points on the graph. The pattern or "scatter" which the points describe suggests types of association of the variables.

The following information indicates the amounts of hours studied per week for ten students and their grade point averages on a scale of 0.00 to 4.00. We are interested in determining whether there is any association between the two variables. In other words, do more hours studied produce higher grades on the average?

Figure 7.10: Hours Studied Per Week and Grade Point Average

STUDENT	HOURS STUDIED (X)	GPA (Y)
A	20	2.9
B	14	2.3
C	17	3.5
D	15	2.1
E	20	3.6
F	19	2.7
G	20	3.1
H	16	2.7
I	23	3.5
J	17	2.6

Using this data, we can construct a scatterplot:

Figure 7.11: Hours Studied and Grade Point Average (GPA)

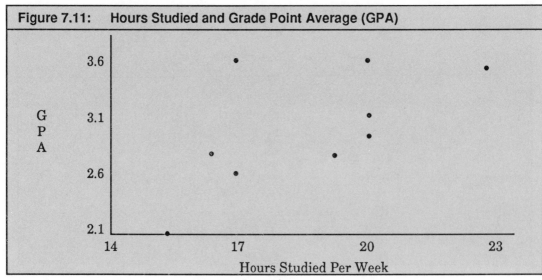

118

You will note that the points tend to line up from lower left to upper right. This tells us that "as hours studied increases, grade point average increases."

Figure 7.11 displays a positive association between two variables. This means that as one increases, so does the other. It is also possible to encounter negative relationships for variables. This means that as one increases, the other decreases. An example of a negative relationship is the average wealth of a neighborhood and the amount of crime in the neighborhood. The higher the wealth, the lower the crime, in general. In some situations, there may be no relationship between variables. In a social program that does not work, for example, the more money spent on the program is unrelated to the improvement in social conditions. In general, money spent on programs to rehabilitate criminals does not lead necessarily to lower crime rates.

Figure 7.12 presents five hypothetical patterns of data on scatterplots. Most scatterplots will resemble one of these patterns. To make an interpretation you need to make a judgment about the pattern of data to determine whether there is a relationship and if so in what direction. Formal statistical calculations can be applied to determine a precise mathematical representation of the pattern of data, but making a judgment is a first step. Once you have done that you will need to calculate a Person's r. A **Pearson's r** is a statistical calculation to give you a number between +1.0 and -1.0 that indicates the relationship between two variables on a scatterplot. A Pearson's r close to +1.0 is a strong positive correlation. One close to -1.0 is a strong negative correlation, and one near 0.0, whether positive or negative, shows little or no correlation.

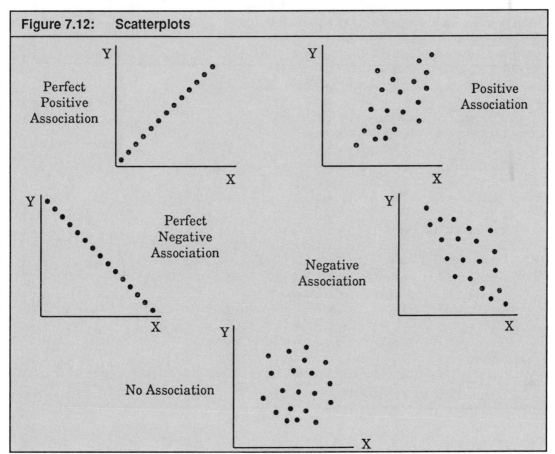

Figure 7.12: Scatterplots

Pearson's r — The Pearson Product Moment Correlation Coefficient

Pearson's r is a correlation statistic, appropriate to interval and ratio scale data. It varies from -1.0 to +1.0. It is possible to express Pearson's r in a form which is easy to calculate:

$$r = \frac{\sum XY - \frac{(\sum X)(\sum Y)}{n}}{\sqrt{\left[\sum X^2 - \frac{(\sum X)^2}{n}\right]\left[\sum Y^2 - \frac{(\sum Y)^2}{n}\right]}}$$

where:

r	=	Pearson's r
n	=	the number of paired observations being tested for association,
X and Y	=	the paired variables
$\sum$	=	sum of all the values of whatever immediately follows this sign

Figure 7.13 shows the calculation of r for the relationship between hours studied and grade point average, using the above formula.

Figure 7.13:   Pearson's r Calculations

After placing the numbers in column x and column y:

Calculation 1	Square each value of X
Calculation 2	Square each value of Y
Calculation 3	Multiply each value of X times Y
Calculation 4	Sum all values of X
Calculation 5	Sum all values of Y
Calculation 6	Sum X^2 values
Calculation 7	Sum Y^2 values
Calculation 8	Sum X x Y values
Calculation 9	From Calculation 8, subtract Calculation 4 x Calculation 5, divided by the number of cases (This is the numerator)
Calculation 10	From Calculation 6, subtract Calculation 4, squared, divided by the number of cases
Calculation 11	From Calculation 7, subtract Calculation 5, squared, divided by the number of cases
Calculation 12	Multiply Calculation 10 x Calculation 11
Calculation 13	Take the square root of Calculation 12
Calculation 14	Divide Calculation 13 into Calculation 9 for the value of Pearson's r.

Figure 7.13 (cont'd): Example of Calculating Pearson's r Calculations

STUDENT	HOURS STUDIED (X)	GPA (Y)	Calc 1 X²	Calc 2 Y²	Calc 3 XY
A	20	2.9	400	8.41	58
B	14	2.3	196	5.29	32.2
C	17	3.5	289	12.25	59.5
D	15	2.1	225	4.41	31.5
E	20	3.6	400	12.96	72
F	19	2.7	361	7.29	51.3
G	20	3.1	400	9.61	62
H	16	2.7	256	7.29	43.2
I	23	3.5	529	12.25	80.5
J	17	2.6	289	6.76	44.2
TOTALS	181	29	3345	86.52	534.4

$$r = \frac{534.4 - \left[\frac{181 \times 29}{10}\right]}{\sqrt{\left[3345 - \frac{181^2}{10}\right]\left[86.52 - \frac{29^2}{10}\right]}}$$

Calc 4   Calc 5   Calc 6   Calc 7   Calc 8

Calculation 9

Calculations 10 & 11

$$r = \frac{534.4 - 524.9}{\sqrt{[(3345 - 3276.1) \times (86.52 - 84.1)]}}$$

Calculation 9
Calculations 10 & 11

$$r = \frac{9.5}{\sqrt{(68.9 \times 2.42)}}$$

Calculation 12

$$r = \frac{9.5}{\sqrt{(166.78)}}$$

Calculation 13

$$r = \frac{9.5}{12.9} = .74$$

Calculation 14

The Pearson's r of .74 is consistent with the upward slope of points on the scatterplot. In other words, there is a strong relationship between hours studied and GPA. For the 10 students in this example, on the average, the more hours studied, the higher the GPA.

121

EXAMPLE

EXERCISE 7.7: USING SCATTERPLOT AND PEARSON'S r

(A) FIND AT LEAST 10 CASES OF TWO INTERVAL VARIABLES. ILLUSTRATE THE RELATIONSHIP BETWEEN THE TWO WITH A SCATTERPLOT. LABEL THE SCATTERPLOT CLEARLY.

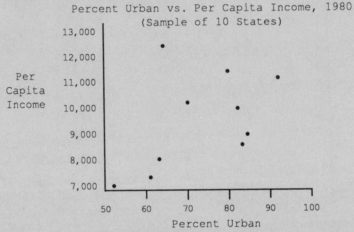

Percent Urban vs. Per Capita Income, 1980
(Sample of 10 States)

SOURCES: PERCENT URBAN POPULATION: U.S. Bureau of the Census, 1980 Census of Population. U.S. Summary. Part A-B, Washington, D.C.: U.S. Government Printing Office, 1982, pp. 51-58
PER CAPITA INCOME: 1982 Information Please Almanac, New York, N.Y.: Simon and Schuster, 1982, p. 37

(B) CALCULATE PEARSON'S r. SHOW YOUR CALCULATIONS.

Percent Urban vs. Per Capita Income
(Sample of 10 States)

CASE	X	Y	X^2	Y^2	XXY
Alabama	60.7	7484	3684.49	56010256	454278.8
Alaska	64.3	12406	4134.49	1.5391e8	797705.8
Arizona	83.8	8649	7022.44	74805201	724786.2
Arkansas	51.6	7180	2662.56	51552400	370488
California	91.3	10856	8335.69	1.1785e8	991152.8
Colorado	80.6	9964	6496.36	99281296	803098.4
Connecticut	78.8	11445	6209.44	1.3099e8	901866
Delaware	70.6	10195	4984.36	1.0394e8	719767
Florida	84.3	8987	7106.49	80766169	757604.1
Georgia	62.4	8000	3893.76	64000000	499200
Sums:	728.4	95166	54530.08	933102944	7019947.

$$\text{Pearson's } r = \frac{7019947 - \dfrac{728.4 \times 95166}{10}}{\sqrt{\left[54530.08 - \dfrac{530566.6}{10}\right]\left[933102944 - \dfrac{9056567556}{10}\right]}}$$

$$= \frac{88055.66}{201096.7}$$

$$= .44$$

(continued)

122

EXAMPLE

EXERCISE 7.7 (continued)

(C) WRITE AN INTERPRETATION OF THE SCATTERPLOT AND THE PEARSON'S r. USE THE PATTERN IN THE PLOT AND THE VALUE OF PEARSON'S r IN THE INTERPRETATION. BRIEFLY SUMMARIZE A MAJOR POINT PORTRAYED AND PROVIDE AN EXPLANATION. IN ADDITION, PROVIDE AN EXAMPLE OF ONE OF THE FOLLOWING: A FORECAST, AN EVALUATION, OR PRESCRIPTION RELATED TO WHAT IS PORTRAYED. CLEARLY LABEL EACH TYPE OF ANALYSIS THAT YOU PROVIDE.

The main point about the sample of 10 states, as shown by the upward slope of the points in the scatterplot, is the positive relationship between the percentage of urban (as opposed to rural) residents and average income. The Pearson's r of .44 indicates that this relationship is moderate. Several factors may help to explain this relationship. One reason is the problems that farmers have in maintaining a level of income comparable to city dwellers, as evidenced by the protests of farmers about their low incomes relative to the rest of society. Since American society is based in part on the goal of equality, the evaluation of this pattern of inequality is that farmers are being treated unfairly by the American economic system.

SUMMARY

DISPLAYS	PURPOSES	EXAMPLES
Scaled Numbers	Report numbers in a way that they are easy to compare and interpret	Number of traffic deaths per 100 million miles travelled in different states
Tables	Compare quantitative information for different years, locations, or other units	Crime rates in different cities for two different periods of time
Bar Graphs	Compare quantitative information for different years, locations, or other units	Compare unemployment rates for regions of the United States
Trend Lines	Show past, present, and future projection of data for periods of time	Size of budget deficits 1975 – 1985
Pie Charts	Show how a quantity is divided into parts	Allocation of tax dollars to different types of government expenditures
Percentage Differences	Show the percent difference between two periods of time, or two locations, or other types of units	Tax receipts increased by 10% between 1983 and 1984 One country's per capita military expenditure is 25% higher than another's
Scatterplot and Pearson's r	Show relationship between two interval variables	Unemployment rate and crime rate is correlated at .55

124

PARTICIPATION ACTIVITY: Providing Numbers and Graphs to Players

1. Select a policy issue that you (or your group) would be interested in studying.

2. Identify a specific player that is interested in the selected issue. Contact the player directly by phone or mail. If you are not sure how to identify and locate the player, review Chapter 6 which provides the necessary information. If you have trouble contacting the actual player or one of the player's assistants, you can still undertake the project and submit it without prior contact. However, it is better to get help from the player at the outset. If you are unable to arrange a meeting, skip the next step and go directly to 4.

3. Explain to the player that you would like to provide a numerical analysis in the form of a display and interpretation. Prepare one or more samples of what you plan to do and show it to the player. Ask for suggestions. Agree on a completion date and the form in which you will submit the final report.

4. Using the guidelines provided in this chapter, prepare a small number of displays and interpretations. Make the displays as professional looking as possible. Each interpretation should include a main point and an explanation. You may also provide a forecast. (An evaluation or prescription may not be appropriate unless the player has agreed on this beforehand.) If you are going to make an oral presentation, or if you think the player may want to use what you produce to make an oral presentation, you should prepare the display on a large board or a transparency for use on an overhead projector.

5. Complete the report on the agreed-upon date, submit it in written form, and offer to make an oral presentation.

6. Thank the player for the opportunity to provide the service. Provide a report to the class on your experience.

PART IV: FORMULATION AND EVALUATION OF PUBLIC POLICY ISSUES

In Part IV, you will formulate and evaluate a public policy on an issue of your choice, and then forecast your policy's effect on the social condition it addresses. First, you will identify a social problem that needs to be addressed. You will then determine what public policy alternative would address that problem. Next, you will identify and measure the benefits and costs of your policy. Finally, you will forecast the impact of your public policy on the social problem it was intended to address.

The seven previous chapters introduced to you basic public policy analysis skills. Beginning with the chapters in this section of the book, and continuing through Part V, you will be expected to conduct a thorough analysis of the single policy issue you have chosen. You will be asked to take a position on this issue—a position based either on your own goals or on the goals of a group that you want to represent.

Chapter 8: Formulating a Position on a Public Policy Issue

Step 1: Identifying the Nature of the Problem

Step 2: Providing Evidence that a Problem Exists

Step 3: Identifying Underlying Factors Contributing to the Problem

Step 4: Describing the Current Policy

Step 5: Developing Public Policy Alternatives and Choosing the Preferred Alternative

Chapter 9: Evaluating Public Policies

Step 1: Identifying Benefits

Step 2: Identifying Costs

Step 3: Collecting Information on Benefits and Costs

Chapter 10: Forecasting the Effect of a Policy with the IMPACT SYSTEM

Step 1: Preparing an Historical Trend Line

Step 2: Making a Baseline Forecast with IMPACT

Step 3: Making a Policy Forecast

CHAPTER 8

FORMULATING A POSITION ON A PUBLIC POLICY ISSUE

YOUR GOAL

To identify a problem that is contributing to a public policy issue, to describe the major factors contributing to the problem, to list public policy alternatives, and to provide a rationale for the alternative you select.

INTRODUCTION

Formulating a position on a public policy issue requires first that you clearly state the problem. Your task continues as you describe, explain, and forecast the social conditions underlying the problem. Next, you must evaluate both the extent to which these conditions need to be improved and the government's role in the action.

To perform these tasks as a public policy analyst, you need to ask the right questions and formulate answers to those questions. It is not possible to know for certain whether the questions and answers you formulate are right until the prescribed policy is implemented; however, your careful application of the steps in this chapter will provide the best possible start.

This chapter introduces five steps in formulating a position on a public policy issue. To acquire the skills in these steps, use the same issue for all five steps.

STEP 8.1
IDENTIFYING THE NATURE OF THE PROBLEM

The first step in formulating a position on a public policy issue is to identify the major problem. A **problem** in policy analysis exists when some members of a community feel social conditions are undesirable. Individuals and groups frequently have different ideas about whether given social conditions are desirable or undesirable. A list of typical problems appears in the figure below.

Figure 8.1: Public Policy Problems at Different Levels

SCHOOL LEVEL

- Low student morale
- High absenteeism
- Poor academic performance
- Vandalism

COMMUNITY LEVEL

- High crime rate
- Deteriorating roads
- Population decline
- Too much commercial development

STATE LEVEL

- Loss of business
- High taxes
- Increased traffic fatalities

NATIONAL LEVEL

- Escalating medical costs
- Decline in exports
- Federal budget deficit

INTERNATIONAL LEVEL

- Famine in Africa
- High debt
- Acid rain

Any public policy issue may be generated by several problems. For example, proposals to reform the federal income tax are stimulated by the reaction of some segments of the society to several conditions including:

- The number of wealthy people paying little or nothing in taxes
- The excessive amount of time necessary to complete a tax form
- The increasing amount of tax evasion
- The unequal distribution of the tax burden on the population

EXAMPLE

EXERCISE 8.1: IDENTIFYING THE NATURE OF THE PROBLEM

BRIEFLY DESCRIBE A PROBLEM. IDENTIFY THE LOCATION OF THE PROBLEM AND TELL WHY THE SOCIAL CONDITIONS ARE UNDESIRABLE:

The problem that needs to be addressed is the large and increased illegal drug use among people eighteen and younger in Riverdale. Some of the undesirable effects of drug use are higher crime rates, poor school performance, worsened health, and even death.

STEP 8.2
PROVIDING EVIDENCE THAT A PROBLEM EXISTS

Just asserting that a problem exists is not an adequate basis for good public policy formulation. You must also provide evidence that the problem exists. The rules indicated in Chapter 3 concerning good monitoring, forecasting, and evaluating should be followed in providing evidence that a problem exists.

Providing the best possible evidence is a difficult task. At the very least, brief case studies that illustrate that the problem exists are necessary. It is better to use sources of data that can be found in written records and, if need be, through factual and attitudinal surveys. Use the skills you learned in Chapters 4, 5, 6, and 7 to acquire and present the evidence necessary to demonstrate that the social conditions actually exist.

In some cases, it is very hard to find clear, identifiable evidence. If the problem is low school morale, for example, there is little clear-cut proof that can be provided to demonstrate the existence of the problem. "Too much commercial development" is difficult to demonstrate, not because data on the amount of commercial development cannot be found, but because what constitutes "too much" is not easily determined. Both of these examples show that such problems should be defined as precisely as possible when identifying the nature of the problem (Step 8.1), so that other analysis steps may be performed.

The need to provide evidence is not only necessary to demonstrate that a problem exists, it also forces the analyst to be clear about identifying the problem. While collecting documented information about the "decline in business in New York State," the problem may become redefined as the "loss of skilled jobs." The narrower definition of the problem might lead to more realistic policy proposals.

It is best to provide evidence drawn from the location of the problem. You can also use supporting evidence from areas that have similar characteristics to the location. Even statewide, national, or international evidence may be cited. If you cite evidence outside the location, you must discuss why it is relevant to your location.

131

EXAMPLE

EXERCISE 8.2: PROVIDING EVIDENCE THAT A PROBLEM EXISTS

PRESENT EVIDENCE THAT A PROBLEM EXISTS. USE THE GUIDELINES FOR MONITORING, FORECASTING, AND EVALUATING SOCIAL CONDITIONS, AS WELL AS STATISTICAL PRESENTATIONS COVERED IN EARLIER CHAPTERS:

Dr. Samuel Smith, Vice Principal of Riverdale High School, states that children as young as ten years of age are now being admitted to rehabilitation programs for chemical dependency.

According to the United States National Institute on Drug Abuse, the percentage of youths who have ever used cocaine rose substantially from 1974 to 1982, and has remained high for marijuana use. While Riverdale usage is probably not as high as national usage, there is no reason to assume that Riverdale is an exception to national trends.

Percentage of Youths Who Have Ever
Used Cocaine or Marijuana (1974,1982)

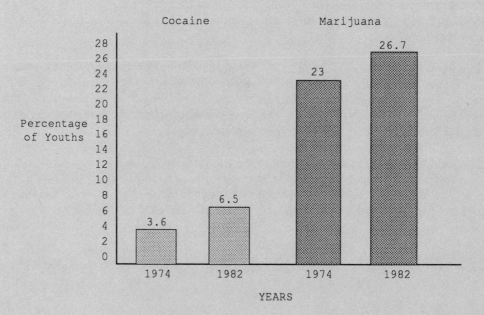

SOURCE: United States National Institute on Drug Abuse as reported in U.S. Department of Commerce, Bureau of the Census. Statistical Abstract of the United States: 1987. (107th ed.) Washington, D.C., 1986. p. 106.

STEP 8.3
IDENTIFYING UNDERLYING FACTORS CONTRIBUTING TO THE PROBLEM

Chapter 3 introduced the idea of explanation as a type of analysis. In this step, you will apply the principles of explanation to identify the reasons or underlying factors behind the problem you have identified and established in Steps 8.1 and 8.2. While the search for social, economic, and political factors can require virtually unlimited amounts of research and never be fully satisfied, you should determine those factors most clearly contributing to the problem.

To illustrate, suppose you are confronted with the problem of a growing number of burglaries in a local community. You might identify as factors contributing to the increase in the number of burglaries:

- understaffed police force
- increased number of wealthy households
- inadequate security precautions
- growing number of young people in the community
- stricter police enforcement in neighboring communities
- increased unemployment in the area
- increased illicit drug usage

Establishing such a list is a start in thinking about possible public policies for dealing with burglaries.

EXAMPLE

EXERCISE 8.3: IDENTIFYING UNDERLYING FACTORS CONTRIBUTING TO THE PROBLEM

BRIEFLY LIST SEVERAL BROAD UNDERLYING FACTORS THAT CONTRIBUTE TO THE PROBLEM THAT YOU HAVE IDENTIFIED:

Drug use is a problem among people 18 and younger for the following reasons:

Readily available drugs

Profitable business for pushers

Broken homes

Peer pressure

Use of drugs by athletes and musicians

Low self-esteem among youths

Pressure from family to succeed

STEP 8.4
DESCRIBING THE CURRENT POLICY

In this step, you will learn how to describe the essential features of one of the major current policies dealing with the social problem you identified in 8.1. As described in Chapter 1, there are three elements of any public policy:

1. *Legislation* to establish general guidelines

2. *Administrative Acts* to establish rules and to distribute funds to put the law into practice

3. *Judicial decisions* to enforce the law and to interpret it in specific situations

Legislation includes both formal laws and agency regulations. For example, at the federal level, Congress establishes guidelines and approves the funding for government actions.

Administrative acts refer to all the activities that government agencies undertake to implement policies. A policy decision to increase police surveillance of roads in order to stop DWI required many detailed decisions. These included the number of police cars, types of cars (marked or unmarked), and surveillance hours and locations. The legislation establishing the policy may require some administrative actions, but agencies almost always are allowed some freedom to make their own decisions in implementing policy.

There are three ways in which any given policy may require the outlay of funds:

- Direct cash outlays (e.g., unemployment checks)
- Purchases of goods or services (e.g., building a bridge)
- Provision of government services (e.g., police surveillance to check for DWI)

Judicial decisions take place when courts make judgments on specific cases. In some decisions, courts must interpret legislative or administrative acts. Legislation and administrative decisions or procedures may be declared unconstitutional if courts determine they violate the United States Constitution.

Examples of Judicial Decisions Shaping Public Policy

The Missouri Compromise, passed by Congress in 1820 to maintain an equal number of free and slave states, was declared unconstitutional in 1857 in *Dred Scott v. Sanford*.

Since the famous Supreme Court case of *Miranda v. Arizona* in 1966, police must advise a suspect of his rights at the time of arrest.

In 1974, in *U.S. v. Nixon*, the Supreme Court held that the President must obey a judge's order to provide evidence needed for a trial.

Judicial decisions can increase or decrease the force of an existing law through the strength of the penalties imposed on violators of those laws. For example, stiffer penalties for DWI, as decided by judges, is part of a policy of cracking down on drunken driving.

When examining any policy, ask the following questions to determine what elements of government actions are involved:

- What legislation underlies the policy?

- What administrative acts have been undertaken to implement the policy? What funds have been expended to implement the policy?

- Has the policy been challenged in court? What kind of penalties have been given to violators of the law?

Information on the legislative, administrative, and judicial aspects of an existing policy can be obtained through library research and by interviewing knowledgeable people. Use the guidelines provided in Chapters 4 and 6 to obtain the information necessary to answer the questions above.

EXAMPLE

EXERCISE 8.4: DESCRIBING THE CURRENT POLICY

(A) DESCRIBE ONE CURRENT POLICY IMPLEMENTED TO REMEDY THE PROBLEM USED IN EXERCISE 8.1:

In Riverdale, one public policy attempting to reduce drug abuse among youths is using the existing family court for drug abuse cases and placing violators on probation. This is an attempt to "shock" the individual away from drugs.

(B) DESCRIBE THE LEGISLATIVE BASIS OF THE POLICY:

New York State has established a family court system to deal with problems involving youths.

(C) DESCRIBE THE ADMINISTRATIVE AND FINANCIAL BASIS OF THE POLICY:

The district attorney has decided to use family courts to deal with some cases of teenage drug abuse. All costs are paid out of regular government funds.

(D) DESCRIBE THE JUDICIAL BASIS OF THE POLICY:

Family court judges have been willing to take drug abuse cases.

STEP 8.5
DEVELOPING PUBLIC POLICY ALTERNATIVES AND CHOOSING THE PREFERRED ALTERNATIVE

Identifying alternative policies is useful because it helps the analyst anticipate both support for and opposition to a proposal. It also forces the analyst to weigh the costs and benefits of different policy prescriptions. Moreover, in the process of developing alternatives, new prescriptions may evolve.

There are several ways to develop public policy alternatives. One way is to look at factors contributing to the problem, as you did in Exercise 8.3. Try selecting one or more major factors and listing alternatives that would lessen the factors. Another way is to make adjustments in current policies. For example, could the current policy which you described in 8.4 be improved?

Once alternatives have been listed, a tentative choice should be made. Two key questions should be asked to make your choice:

1. Which policy is most likely to be accepted by those who will determine whether or not the policy is implemented? (Feasibility)

2. Which alternative appears to have the maximum beneficial impact with the minimum cost? (Effectiveness)

It is ideal to find policies that are highly feasible and highly effective, but this almost never happens in the real world. Usually it is necessary to choose among policies that have some attractive features in both feasibility and effectiveness.

The following example shows how feasibility and effectiveness should be weighed to select the best of three alternatives aimed at reducing DWI:

Example of How to Weigh Feasibility and Effectiveness

Alternative Policies for Reducing DWI:

1. Establish a federal drinking age of 21 years old. (AGE)
2. Make all new cars sold have a feature where the driver must pass a breathalizer test in order to start the car. (TEST)
3. Make the consumption of alcohol illegal. (CONS)

		Feasibility		
		HIGH	MEDIUM	LOW
	HIGH		AGE	CONS
Effectiveness	MEDIUM			TEST
	LOW			

The 21-year-old drinking age is the preferred choice because it is more feasible than the other two and is at least as effective as the other two. It has medium feasibility because it is already the law in many states. It is highly effective because it does reduce the number of DWI arrests where it is the law. Testing has a medium level of effectiveness, because it would slightly reduce the number of drunken drivers. Because of its extremely high cost, it is low on feasibility. Making consumption illegal is high on effectiveness because it would reduce the number of drunk drivers. However, it is low on feasibility; prohibition was already tried in this country and was very unpopular.

Although you do not have to present the diagram in completing Exercise 8.5, you should use it to assess the three alternatives you consider. You will find it useful to draw it and place the three alternatives in the appropriate cells to help you develop your reasoning for selecting the preferred alternative.

EXAMPLE

EXERCISE 8.5: DEVELOPING PUBLIC POLICY ALTERNATIVES AND CHOOSING THE PREFERRED ALTERNATIVE

PROVIDE AT LEAST THREE PROPOSED PUBLIC POLICY ALTERNATIVES TO DEAL WITH THE PROBLEM YOU HAVE IDENTIFIED AT THE SAME LOCATION IN 8.1. EACH ALTERNATIVE MUST SPECIFY THE ACTUAL GOVERNMENT OR GOVERNMENT AGENCY THAT WILL CARRY OUT THE PROPOSED ACTION. INDICATE WHICH PROPOSAL YOU THINK IS MOST PROMISING BY LISTING IT FIRST. DISCUSS WHY YOU CONSIDER IT TO BE THE PREFERRED CHOICE OVER THE OTHER TWO:

Three possible proposals for attacking the drug problem among the youths eighteen and younger are:

1) A community teen court to sentence young drug offenders to hours of community service, not time in jail

2) Increased education in grade schools about drugs and their effects

3) A program that uses undercover narcotics agents in public high schools

Neither increased education nor the use of undercover narcotics agents are likely to have much of an impact on drug usage among teenagers. Existing educational programs have not proved very effective and more programs are not likely to either. The use of undercover narcotics agents would only push the drug problem outside school and do little to reduce drug usage among teenagers. It would also be opposed by important players in the community. The community teen court would not eliminate the drug problem, but it could use peer pressure to reduce it significantly. In addition, it is likely to be supported by most key players in the community because it is a new approach and does not involve significant public spending.

SUMMARY

CONCEPTS	DEFINITIONS	TASKS	EXAMPLES
Problem	Social conditions which some members of a community feel are undesirable	Identify the problems underlying a public policy issue	High automobile fatality rate
Evidence of a Problem	Information that documents the existence of undesirable social conditions	Collect and display research findings	Trend line displaying automobile fatality rate
Factors Contributing to the Problem	Conditions affecting a problem	Collect and display research findings	Alcohol consumption related to automobile fatalities
Current Policy	Government actions currently being implemented to deal with the problem	Describe the current policy and the legislation, administrative acts, and judicial decisions related to it	Increased police surveillance to stop DWI
Preferred Policy Alternative	Best policy (based on effectiveness and feasibility) from a list of proposals	List alternatives and indicate why one is preferred over the others	Raising the drinking age is preferred over prohibition to decrease DWI because they both have high effectiveness, but the latter has a lower feasibility

141

PARTICIPATION ACTIVITY: Providing a Formulation to Players

1. Select a policy issue that you (or your group) would be interested in studying.

2. Identify a specific player that is interested in the selected issue. Contact the player directly, by phone or mail. If you are not sure how to identify and locate the player, review Chapter 6, which provides the necessary information. If you have trouble contacting the actual player or one of the player's assistants, you can still undertake the project and submit it without prior contact. However, it is better to get help from the player at the outset. If you are unable to arrange a meeting, skip the next step and go directly to 4.

3. Explain that you would like to provide policy suggestions to the player pertaining to a specific social problem. Provide a brief overview of your general ideas and ask for suggestions. Indicate when you expect to send the report.

4. Write a report that follows the general outline of this chapter. A statement of the problem (see Step 8.1) should be in your introductory paragraph. Each of the next four sections should cover the material for each of the remaining steps in the chapter. A summary of your entire paper, called an "Executive Summary," should appear at the beginning of the paper. The paper should conform to the outline below:

   Executive Summary
   Introduction
   Evidence of Problem
   Contributing Factors
   Existing Policies
   Suggested Policies

   If you have limited time or the player expresses a specific interest, you may only want to complete one or two parts (most likely evidence of the problem or suggested policies).

5. Complete the report on the agreed-upon date, submit it in written form, and offer to make an oral presentation.

6. Thank the player for the opportunity to provide the service. Provide a report to the class on your experience.

CHAPTER 9

EVALUATING PUBLIC POLICIES

YOUR GOAL

To identify and measure the benefits and costs of a policy.

INTRODUCTION

The previous chapter discussed formulating public policy. This chapter examines the tasks you must perform once the policy has been implemented. Evaluation is an essential task of public policy analysis because it measures the effectiveness of the policy selected. Unfortunately, it is a task not frequently carried out in a systematic way. Usually, policy-makers are so consumed in debating which policies to follow and then in implementing the selected policies, that they do not have the time or energy to assess the impact of the policy itself.

It is essential that public policy analysts develop skills in evaluating policies. Failure to evaluate policies is bad for several reasons:

- Policies that do not work may be continued
- Policies that do work may be abandoned
- Potential lessons from our mistakes are lost
- Policy-makers are not held accountable for what they do

This chapter introduces you to the first tasks in the process of evaluating public policy: identifying and thinking about how to measure the benefits and costs of the policy. The skills you acquire in this chapter prepare you for beginning a policy evaluation study if and when your policy is implemented.

143

STEP 9.1
IDENTIFYING BENEFITS

Benefits are consequences of a policy which are considered by the analyst to be good for the society or some segment of it. For example, the primary benefits of mandatory seatbelt laws are fewer fatalities and injuries to those involved in automobile accidents.

Benefits can be tangible, usually expressed in the form of dollars or other numbers. For example, seatbelt laws might eventually reduce car insurance by an average of $30 to $50 per year, and decrease fatalities about 10%. They can also be intangible and hard to measure concretely. For example, drivers and passengers may feel more secure wearing seatbelts. Both tangible and intangible benefits are important to consider in evaluating an existing or proposed public policy.

Three sources of benefits are:

- The **action** itself
- The **intended consequences** of the policy
- The **unintended consequences** of the policy

The first category applies only when the policy itself represents a benefit. Intended and unintended consequences are less easy to identify. Intended consequences are, in effect, the goals of the policy. Unintended consequences result from intended consequences, although they are not the major reason for the policy.

Example of Benefits of a Policy

The city government decides to take action against increased vandalism by youths. It implements a policy of hiring 100 youths to patrol the city parks. The benefits include:

- The action itself—the 100 jobs
- The intended consequence of the policy—reduction of vandalism
- The unintended consequence of the policy—increased enjoyment of the park by more people as the fear of vandalism is reduced

---

144

EXAMPLE

EXERCISE 9.1: IDENTIFYING BENEFITS

(A) STATE YOUR PREFERRED POLICY:

Implement a Community Teen Court

(B) IDENTIFY THE THREE MOST IMPORTANT BENEFITS:

1. The teens will receive counselling and rehabilitation.

2. The teens will abstain from drug usage.

3. Teen vandalism in the community will decrease.

STEP 9.2
IDENTIFYING COSTS

Costs are consequences of a policy which are negative for the society as a whole or some segment of it. For example, the primary costs of the mandatory seatbelt laws are a loss of freedom of choice for drivers and passengers, and more law enforcement expenditures.

Costs, like benefits, can be tangible, usually expressed in the form of dollars or other numbers. For example, a community's budget for additional law enforcement may increase by $10,000, a 2% increase. They can also be intangible and hard to measure concretely. For example, more hostile attitudes toward government may result from the seatbelt requirement. Both tangible and intangible costs are important to consider in evaluating an existing or proposed public policy.

Costs have the same three sources as benefits:

- The **action** itself
- The **intended consequences**
- The **unintended consequences**

Example of Costs of a Policy

In taking the action of employing 100 youths to patrol the city parks, the city government will incur costs, in addition to the benefits cited in Step 9.1. The costs include:

- The action itself— cost of paying the salary of the youths
- The intended consequence—need to hire additional staff to supervise the 100 new employees
- The unintended consequence—more litter and increased wear and tear on the park from increased usage

---

In some cases, costs can be the opposite of the originally forecasted benefits. For example, because people are wearing seatbelts, they may feel overly secure and drive more recklessly. The resulting cost may be increased traffic deaths instead of the expected reduction in traffic deaths.

Example of Costs Being Opposite of Planned Benefits

In the policy of hiring 100 youths to patrol the city parks, a planned benefit was reduction of vandalism in the parks. However, vandalism could increase because some of the hired youths could take advantage of their access to the park and increase the vandalism.

146

EXAMPLE

EXERCISE 9.2: IDENTIFYING COSTS

(A) STATE YOUR PREFERRED POLICY:

Implement a Community Teen Court

(B) IDENTIFY THE THREE MOST IMPORTANT COSTS:

1. Fewer volunteers for other organizations

2. More teenage drug use, because teen courts may appear to be very lenient

3. Cost for staff member to administer the court

147

STEP 9.3
COLLECTING INFORMATION ON BENEFITS AND COSTS

Once the benefits and costs have been identified, the next step is to determine how you can collect information to measure them. To do this, you will need to do the following:

1. Determine the most precise way of measuring each benefit and cost.

2. Locate data sources that provide the necessary information.

Some benefits and costs can be precisely defined. Costs measured in dollars or person-hours of work that are part of the implementation of the policy can clearly be identified and, assuming records are kept, be measured. Statistics that measure social conditions that are a consequence of the policy can also be used. For the mandatory seatbelt law in New York State, statistics can be gathered on the number of traffic fatalities. Where less tangible benefits and costs are identified, such as loss of individual freedom, measurement is more difficult. In cases where you cannot obtain published information or conduct a formal survey, you can still obtain estimates from experts.

Once you have defined the benefits and costs as precisely as you can, use your library and survey research skills covered in Chapters 4, 5, and 6 to collect the necessary information.

EXAMPLE

EXERCISE 9.3: COLLECTING
INFORMATION ON BENEFITS AND COSTS

(A) STATE YOUR PREFERRED POLICY:

Establish a Community Teen Court

(B) IDENTIFY AN IMPORTANT BENEFIT AND COST FOR YOUR PREFERRED POLICY AND NEXT TO EACH ONE, DESCRIBE HOW YOU WOULD MEASURE IT AND WHAT YOUR SOURCE OF DATA WOULD BE:

BENEFIT: HOW MEASURED AND SOURCE OF DATA:

Decrease in teen   Number of drug abuse cases reported by the
drug abuse in the   police
community

COST: HOW MEASURED AND SOURCE OF DATA:

Fewer volunteers for   Assessed by means of reports from volunteer
other organizations   organizations

SUMMARY

CONCEPTS	DEFINITIONS	TASKS	EXAMPLES
Benefits	Desirable consequences of a public policy	List major benefits of a policy	Fewer people on welfare is a benefit of a policy of hiring more government employees from the welfare rolls
Costs	Undesirable consequences of a public policy	List major costs of a policy	Increased number of homeless persons is a cost of a policy to cut government housing subsidies

PARTICIPATION ACTIVITY: Providing an Evaluation to Players

1. Select a policy issue that you (or your group) would be interested in studying.

2. Identify a specific player that is interested in the selected issue. Contact the player directly by phone or mail. If you are not sure how to identify and locate the player, review Chapter 6, which provides the necessary information. If you have trouble contacting the actual player or one of the player's assistants, you can still undertake the project and submit it without prior contact. However, it is better to get help from the player at the outset. If you are unable to arrange a meeting, skip the next step and go directly to 4.

3. Explain to the player that you would like to conduct an evaluation of an existing policy or to design a study for evaluating a proposed public policy should it be implemented. Ask for information on the benefits and costs that the player thinks have or might result from the policy. Also ask for suggestions on where additional relevant information might be found.

4. Produce a report that begins with a discussion of the benefits and costs of the existing or proposed policy. For an existing policy, prepare a report that has the following outline:

   Executive Summary
   Key Benefits and Costs
   Historical Information on Benefits and Costs

   For a proposed policy, prepare a report that has the following outline:

   Executive Summary
   Key Benefits and Costs
   Historical Information on Benefits and Costs
   Forecasts of Benefits and Costs With and Without the Policy

5. Complete the report on the agreed-upon date, submit it in written form, and offer to make an oral presentation.

6. Thank the player for the opportunity to provide the service. Provide a report to the class on your experience.

CHAPTER 10

FORECASTING THE EFFECT OF A POLICY WITH THE IMPACT SYSTEM

YOUR GOAL

To prepare a forecast of the impact of your policy on the social condition your policy addresses.

INTRODUCTION

Having reached this point, you have already isolated the key benefits and costs that your preferred public policy is intended to produce. You now begin the important task of forecasting whether or not the policy you have proposed will produce the desired changes in social conditions. The next three steps provide the tools for beginning that evaluation by forecasting the possible effects of your policy in terms of benefits and costs. By carefully estimating which social conditions will change (and which will not change), you form the basis for evaluating your proposed policy after it is implemented.

The three steps in this chapter are:

1. **Preparing an historical trend line** of a social condition (a benefit or cost) that you believe will be affected by your proposed policy.

2. **Developing a baseline forecast,** that is, a forecast of how the selected social condition will change if your policy is not implemented.

3. **Developing a policy forecast,** by adjusting the baseline forecast to reflect how the social condition you select will be affected if the policy is implemented.

STEP 10.1
PREPARING AN HISTORICAL TREND LINE

CHOOSE A KEY BENEFIT OR COST

Begin this step by deciding which benefit or cost you wish to study. To do this, you can build on what you have learned from Chapter 9. If you were to do a complete evaluation, you would study the historical trends and forecasts of all the key benefits and costs. However, for exercise 10.1, you will need to select just one of the benefits or costs. When you select the benefit or cost, define your choice in measurable terms and indicate your data source (as you did in Step 9.3). Defining a measurement for a benefit or cost creates a **variable**.

**Example of Defining a Variable from the Proposed
Mandatory Automobile Air Bag Law**

The proposed policy is that all automobile manufacturers be required to install air bags that instantly inflate when an automobile is involved in a crash. One of the intended key benefits of this policy is the reduction of the rate of highway fatalities. To create a variable, this benefit is defined as the number of traffic deaths per 100 million miles driven.

MEASURING THE TREND

Before a forecast can be made, you will need to record and display the history of your variable. The most efficient way to present this historical information for the purpose of evaluation is to display the variable (the measured benefit or cost) in a trend line. You may wish to review Step 7.4 for the way to construct such a graph. Include in your graph historical data that is as close to the present time as possible. Because most historical information does not become published until it is a year or two old, you may be unable to obtain official figures for the most recent years. In that case, provide estimates. Indicate an estimate by placing an "E" following the date on the horizontal axis of the graph. When you complete this step, your graph should look like the one in Figure 10.1, which includes variables through 1987. The graph was completed at the beginning of 1988. You should follow this same model: include variables (estimated if necessary) up to the year just prior to the current year in which you are preparing the graph. Indicate the published sources or basis of the estimate for each time period. Also calculate two averages, one for all five years, and one for the two most recent years. These averages will be used later in making the forecasts.

The following example shows a clear statement of a key indicator of the success of a proposed national air bag policy. It includes the historical trend, estimated where necessary, the sources of actual data, and an explanation of estimates that are made.

154

Figure 10.1: Historical Trend Line Prepared for Measuring a Key Benefit or Cost of a Proposed Policy

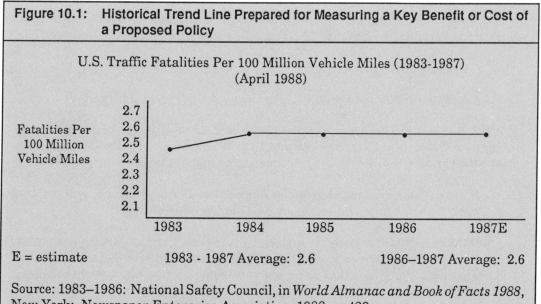

U.S. Traffic Fatalities Per 100 Million Vehicle Miles (1983-1987)
(April 1988)

E = estimate   1983 - 1987 Average: 2.6   1986–1987 Average: 2.6

Source: 1983–1986: National Safety Council, in *World Almanac and Book of Facts 1988*, New York: Newspaper Enterprise Association, 1988, p. 423.
1987: Estimated. Although the actual number of deaths has increased, the total number of miles driven has increased as well. Therefore, the death rate should remain about the same as in the previous year.

In Figure 10.1 the variables for 1983 through 1986 were taken from a published source. As is commonly the case, the information for the most recent year, (1987) was not available when the chart was prepared (mid-1988). Therefore an estimate for 1987 had to be made. The estimate of 2.6 deaths per 100 million miles driven was based on the assumption that the trend between 1985 and 1986 would continue into 1987, and that the death rate would stay about the same.

Note that historical information was presented for the five years preceding 1988, the year when the policy is assumed to be implemented. On some occasions, shorter time periods than a year might be used. For example, for education policies, you might use semesters. A time series of ten or more years would be an even sounder base for evaluating and forecasting. Whatever the time period covered, when creating an historic trend line, use a minimum of five time periods.

One thing you will need as a basis of your forecast is an historical average of the past values of the variable. In Exercise 10.1 you will compute two historical averages:

- A five-year historical average

- A two-year historical average, using the two most recent time periods

After that, you will choose one of these historical averages as the starting point for making your forecasts in Exercises 10.2 and 10.3. Which one you choose depends on the pattern the variable shows over the full time period, using the following guidelines:

- If the variable does not show a clear upward or downward trend, or if it shows more than one high and low value, use the five-year average.

- If the variable is consistently increasing over time, like the growing percentage of women in the armed forces (Figure 7.2), use the two-year historical average. The reason for this is that using the average for all five years would produce a number that was too low. When the trend is strongly upward the more recent values are a better basis for a forecast. For example, the five-year average of the percentage of women in the armed forces is 7.6. On the other hand, the two-year average is 9.4, which is much closer to the more recent levels.

- If the variable is consistently decreasing over time, use the two-year historical average. In this case as well, the more recent values will be a better basis of your forecast.

- If the variable shows an upward or downward trend, but also has some ups and downs, the decision is difficult. When in doubt, choose the five-year average, since this is a way of using all the scores of the variables as part of your forecast.

The example of Exercise 10.1 shows some ups and downs, as well as a trend, leaving the student in doubt; in this case the five-year historical average was selected.

On the next page is the Example for Exercise 10.1, showing the trend of one of the key variables of the proposed Teen Court—the number of drug-related arrests among teen-agers.

156

EXAMPLE

EXERCISE 10.1: PREPARING AN HISTORICAL TREND LINE

(A) CONSTRUCT A TREND LINE THAT INCLUDES A MINIMUM OF FIVE TIME PERIODS FOR A KEY BENEFIT OR COST OF YOUR POLICY. PROVIDE TITLES AND LABELLING.

TITLE: Number of Drug-Related Arrests of Teen-Agers Reported by the Riverdale Police (1983-1987)

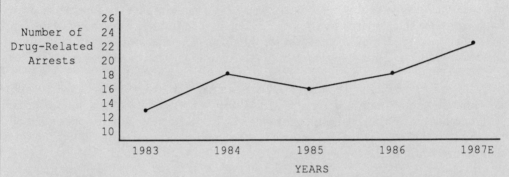

E=estimate

(B) INDICATE THE SOURCES OR RATIONALE FOR EACH TIME PERIOD:

TIME PERIODS	VALUE	SOURCE OR RATIONALE
1983	14	Riverdale police department records, reported in the February 20, 1988 issue of *Riverdale Times*, p. 1
1984	18	"
1985	16	"
1986	17	"
1987	22	Estimate. The published figures included 1987 data from January through October 1987. During this 10-month period there were 18 incidents, an average of 1.8 per month. The estimate for 1987 was made by multiplying 12 x 1.8.

(C) CALCULATE THE FIVE-YEAR HISTORICAL AVERAGE AND THE TWO-YEAR HISTORICAL AVERAGE, INDICATE WHICH IS A BETTER BASIS FOR A FORECAST, AND BRIEFLY GIVE THE REASON FOR THE ONE YOU CHOOSE.

FIVE-YEAR HISTORICAL AVERAGE: 17.4
TWO-YEAR HISTORICAL AVERAGE: 19.5

CHOICE AND RATIONALE: I choose the five-year historical average because the variable shows both some ups and downs and some trend; since the overall pattern is not clear, I chose the five-year average in order to include all values of the variable.

157

STEP 10.2
MAKING A BASELINE FORECAST WITH IMPACT

By this point you have selected a variable that you wish to forecast and prepared a trend line of how that variable has varied over the past five years. You are now ready to make a baseline forecast. A **baseline forecast** is a forecast of what will happen to your selected social condition assuming that the policy you have proposed is *not* implemented. In this section, we will provide you with a forecasting tool called **Impact**. It will enable you to make a five-year average forecast so that you can compare the forecast of the next five years with the previous five years. The choice of a five-year average is done for the sake of simplicity. It would be more useful to have a forecast of the variable for each of the next five years. That, however, would require methods beyond the scope of this book.

A forecast variable will compare to the past in one of three ways—it will be higher, lower, or the same. Impact, described in this step, is a way to forecast whether the trend will increase, decrease, or remain the same. To begin Impact, first prepare a list of the most important factors that will determine the trend of your variable. Select the Impact factors according to the following guidelines:

1. Select the most essential social, economic, and political conditions that influence the variable you will be forecasting.

2. Select factors that increase or decrease over time. This is especially important for government policy, which may be included as a factor only if the policy is defined as the amount of government expenditures or as some other quantitative measure.

3. Select factors likely to be affected by the policy you have proposed. For example, one of the factors included in the forecast of the traffic death rate, in Figure 10.2, is the number of safety features on automobiles, which is directly related to the mandatory air bag policy.

When you have listed the factors, provide two estimates for each one: (1) the type of impact the factor has on the variable you have chosen; and (2) the likely future trend of the factor.

Study the Impact Information Worksheet appearing in Figure 10.2. On the information page are listed the five major factors that influence the variable to be forecast. Each factor has been assigned two numbers: (1) the impact of the factor on the forecast variable, and (2) the trend of the factor.

1. *Impact of Factor on Forecast Variable* — this number estimates whether the factor contributes to a higher or lower forecast variable. For example, studies show that as speed limits increase, traffic fatalities increase. If you were using speed limits as a factor to forecast traffic fatalities, you would assign a positive number (+1, +2, or +3) to this factor. A positive number indicates that if the factor increases, the forecast variable increases; if the factor decreases, the forecast variable decreases. The numbers from 1 to 3 indicate how important the factor is in determining the forecast variable. A 1 means low impact, 2 moderate impact, and 3 a high impact. In the case of the impact of speed limits on traffic fatalities, a +3 is a reasonable estimate, since studies show a clear and direct correlation between speed limits and fatalities. The number of young drivers is another factor with a positive relationship with traffic fatalities; the more young drivers, the more fatalities. In this case, however, the correlation is not so strong, and so a +1 would be a more reasonable estimate.

You might also use the degree of speed limit enforcement as one factor to forecast traffic fatalities. Enforcement is an example of a factor with a negative relationship to traffic deaths. A negative relationship means that if the factor increases, the variable decreases; if the factor decreases, the variable increases. If you were using the degree of enforcement to forecast traffic fatalities you would assign a negative number (-1, -2, or -3). As with positive relationships, 1, 2, and 3 stand for low, medium, and high impact, respectively. You might reasonably assign a -3 for the impact of the size of the police force on the crime rate since there is generally a very strong negative relationship between the size of the police force and the level of crime rates.

Do not assign a 0 to the relationship. If a factor has neither a positive nor a negative impact on the forecast variable, do not include the factor in your list.

2. *Trend of Factor* — this number may be +1, +2, or +3 to indicate how the trend of the factor itself will increase in the future; or it may be -1, -2, or -3 to indicate how the factor trend will decrease in the future. You may also assign a 0 if you believe the factor trend will neither increase nor decrease.

In addition to assigning numbers to each of the five factors mentioned, also provide a brief rationale or reasoning behind your estimates for the numbers you have assigned. Provide a rationale for each impact number and each trend number. Figure 10.2 shows an example of the factors and their impact and trend estimates for forecasting the rate of traffic deaths.

Figure 10.2: Impact Information Worksheet
Factors and Rationales Used in Making a Baseline Forecast

Forecast Variable: *U.S. Traffic Deaths per 100 Million Vehicle Miles*

FACTOR 1   *State speed limits*   RATIONALE

Impact of
the Factor   *+3*   Many studies have shown the relationship between higher speeds and higher death rates.

Trend of
the Factor   *+1*   Because of a change in federal law, many states are raising their speed limits, which will lead to higher average driving speeds.

FACTOR 2   *Degree of speed limit enforcement*

Impact of
the Factor   *-2*   Stricter enforcement of speed laws would decrease the death rate.

Trend of
the Factor   *0*   Enforcement is unlikely to increase at the same time that limits are increased.

FACTOR 3   *Safety features on automobiles*

Impact of
the Factor   *-3*   The greater the number of safety features on automobiles, the lower the death rate.

Trend of
the Factor   *+1*   Because of federal laws, automakers are likely to continue to add safety features on new automobiles.

FACTOR 4   *Number of young drivers*

Impact of
the Factor   *+1*   Younger drivers have higher death rates than older drivers.

Trend of
the Factor   *0*   The number of younger drivers will remain constant over the next five years.

FACTOR 5   *Number of people wearing seatbelts*

Impact of
the Factor   *-3*   According to the January 1987 issue of *Police Chief*, 10,000 lives could be saved if people would wear their seatbelts.

Trend of
the Factor   *0*   The number of people wearing seatbelts is not increasing, according to the same issue of *Police Chief*.

160

Once you have estimated the values for each of the five factors, you are ready to calculate the average for the five year forecast. In the Impact Calculation Worksheet (Figure 10.3) that follows, you will note that we have placed the numbers from the Impact Information Worksheet that were assigned for Factor Impact and Factor Trend. The calculation process is described in the example that follows.

Figure 10.3: Impact Calculation Worksheet

Calculation 1: Impact of Factor x Trend of Factor = Impact Score. For each of the five factors, multiply the assigned impact number by the assigned trend number. For example, for Factor One, the Impact score is a +3, resulting from the product of +3 x +1. If the trend is 0, the number assigned the impact factor (without regard to whether it has a + or - sign) becomes the Impact score. It should be placed in parenthesis to indicate the impact score has no sign.

Calculation 2: Sum of all Positive Impact Scores Plus 1/2 Zero-Trend Impact Scores. Find the sum of all the positive scores plus 1/2 of scores in parenthesis. For example, the sum of the positive and 1/2 the zero-trend scores for the traffic fatality example is 6.

Calculation 3: Sum of All Scores Ignoring Signs and Parentheses. Find the sum of all the scores ignoring signs and parentheses. For example, the sum for this example is 12.

Calculation 4: Divide Calculation 2 by Calculation 3. Divide Calculation 2 by Calculation 3. For example, the calculation for this example is .50.

Calculation 5: Calculation 4 + .50. To the number you obtained in Calculation 4, add the constant value, .50. For example, Calculation 4 resulted in a value of .50. Add .50 to this for a score of 1.0. In general, when Calculation 4 is greater than .50, the result will be greater than 1.0. When Calculation 4 is less than .50, the result will be less than 1.0. When Calculation 4 is exactly .50, the result will be exactly 1.0.

Calculation 6: Calculation 5 x the Historical Average You Have Chosen. Use the historical average (five-year or two-year) that you selected in Exercise 10.1, and multiply it by the number obtained in Calculation 5. For example, the five-year historical average from Figure 10.1 was 2.6 and Calculation 5 resulted in a value of 1.0. Therefore, the five-year forecast is 2.6. In general, when Calculation 5 is greater than 1.0, the five-year forecast will be higher than the historical average. When it is less than 1.0, the five-year forecast will be less than the historical average. When it is exactly 1.0, the forecast will be exactly the same as the historical average.

Below are the calculations completed to create the forecast of traffic deaths for the next five years.

Factors, Estimates, and Calculations for Making the Baseline Forecast

Calculation 1

Factor	Impact (-3 to +3)	Trend (-3 to +3)	Impact Scores
1. Speed limits	+3	+1	+3
2. Enforcement	-2	0	(2)
3. Safety devices	-3	+1	-3
4. Young drivers	+1	0	(1)
5. Seatbelt wearers	-3	0	(3)

Calculation 2: Sum of positive scores plus 1/2 of scores in parentheses = 6
Calculation 3: Sum of scores ignoring signs and parentheses = 12
Calculation 4: Calculation 2 divided by Calculation 3 = .50
Calculation 5: Calculation 4 + .50 = 1.0
Calculation 6: Calculation 5   x   Historical average   = 5-year base forecast
                              1.0   x   2.6   =   2.6

162

The Impact procedure gives you a conservative forecast, somewhere between .5 of the (two-year or five-year) historical average, and 1.5 of the previous average. Sometimes variables may increase more or less than this; however, this approach gives you a general sense of the trend of the variable, based on the factors you have identified.

On the following page are the worksheets for preparing a baseline forecast concerning the drug-related arrests of teenagers, as a step toward evaluating the implementation of a Teen Court in Riverdale.

EXAMPLE

EXERCISE 10.2: MAKING A BASELINE FORECAST

(A) INDICATE YOUR FORECAST VARIABLE, AT LEAST THREE OF THE MOST IMPORTANT SOCIAL, ECONOMIC, AND POLITICAL FACTORS THAT INFLUENCE THE FORECAST VARIABLE, THE IMPACT OF THE FACTOR AND THE FUTURE FIVE-YEAR TREND OF THE FACTOR. PROVIDE A RATIONALE OF EACH IMPACT ESTIMATE AND EACH TREND ESTIMATE:

FORECAST VARIABLE: Number of drug-related arrests of teenagers

FACTOR 1 Police crackdown on drug pushers

IMPACT OF
THE FACTOR   -1   Police investigations of drug sales have had a limited ability to deter drug use in the past according to a previous study cited in the Riverdale Times.

TREND OF
THE FACTOR   0   Because of budget limitations, the police will not be able to step up their surveillance of drug users.

FACTOR 2 Number of teenagers

IMPACT OF
THE FACTOR   +2   Since teenagers are an active group of drug-users, the size of the teenage population tends to lead to higher drug use.

TREND OF
THE FACTOR   0   In Riverdale the number of teenagers will neither increase nor decrease.

FACTOR 3 Number of teenagers sentenced for drug use

IMPACT OF
THE FACTOR   -3   The publicity associated with sentencing for drug-abuse is one of the best deterrents.

TREND OF
THE FACTOR   -2   Because of the inattention of the police, and because of enormous demands on the court system, the number of sentences will decrease.

FACTOR 4 Drug availability

IMPACT OF
THE FACTOR   +3   The supply of drugs is one of the chief factors leading to more drug abuse.

TREND OF
THE FACTOR   +3   The supply of drugs, at lower cost, will continue to increase rapidly in the community.

FACTOR 5 Education programs

IMPACT OF
THE FACTOR   -1   Education programs, on television and in the schools, have a slight tendency to decrease drug abuse.

TREND OF
THE FACTOR   +1   The number of such education programs will increase, both among the public and in the schools.

(continued)

EXERCISE 10.2 (continued)

(B) LIST FACTORS AND ESTIMATES IN THE CHART BELOW AND COMPLETE THE INDICATED CALCULATIONS:

FACTOR	IMPACT (-3 TO +3)	TREND (-3 TO +3)	CALCULATION 1 IMPACT SCORES
1. Police crackdown	-1	0	(1)
2. No. of teens	+2	0	(2)
3. No. of sentences	-3	-2	+6
4. Drug availability	+3	+3	+9
5. Education programs	-1	+1	-1

CALCULATION 2: Sum of positive scores plus 1/2 of scores in parentheses = 16.5
CALCULATION 3: Sum of scores ignoring signs and parentheses = 19
CALCULATION 4: Calculation 2 divided by Calculation 3 = .87
CALCULATION 5: Calculation 4 + .5 = 1.37
CALCULATION 6: Calculation 5   x   Historical average   = 5-year baseline forecast
      1.37   x   17.40   = 23.81 drug-related arrests per year average over next five years

STEP 10.3
MAKING A POLICY FORECAST

Now that you have summarized the historical trend and generated a five-year baseline forecast, you are ready to forecast the impact of your proposed policy on the key benefit or cost that you have selected to study. The policy you have selected ought to have impact on one or more of the Impact Factors included in the analysis you completed in Step 10.2. Thoroughly analyze the possible impact of the policy on both the impact and trend of each of the five factors included in your analysis. Provide a rationale for each changed number. The following figure shows the revised estimates for the air bag law.

Figure 10.4: Making a Policy Forecast For Impact of Air Bag Law on Fatalities

A. Factors and estimates used in baseline forecast, and changes expected as a result of implementation of proposed policy.

Factor	Baseline Forecast Estimates		New Estimates (If Different)		Reasons For Differences
	Impact	Trend	Impact	Trend	
1. Speed limit	+3	+1	same	same	
2. Enforcement	-2	0	same	same	
3. Safety devices	-3	+1	same	+2	The required air-bags will make cars much safer.
4. Young drivers	+1	0	same	same	
5. Seatbelt wearers	-3	0	-2	same	The proposed policy will make seatbelt wearing less important in the death rate.

B. Policy forecast calculations based on revised estimates

Factor	Impact (-3 to +3)	Trend (-3 to +3)	Impact Scores
1. Speed limits	+3	+1	+3
2. Enforcement	-2	0	(2)
3. Safety devices	-3	+2	-6
4. Young drivers	+1	0	(1)
5. Seatbelt wearers	-2	0	(2)

CALCULATION 2: Sum of positive scores plus 1/2 of scores in parentheses =5.5
CALCULATION 3: Sum of scores ignoring signs and parentheses   = 14
CALCULATION 4: Calculation 2 divided by Calculation 3   = .39
CALCULATION 5: Calculation 4 + .50   = .89
CALCULATION 6: Calculation 5x Historical average = 5-year policy forecast
$$\underline{.89} \quad \times \quad \underline{2.6} \quad = \underline{2.3}$$

Finally, the new policy forecast from the Impact Chart is used to amend the historic trend line graph as produced in Exercise 10.1. As the example shows, indicated on the trend line are the three averages: the average of the past five years, the baseline forecast average, and the policy forecast average. (Use the five-year historical average for comparison even if you used the two-year historical average in your forecast.) The figure below shows these analyses for the effects of the air bag law.

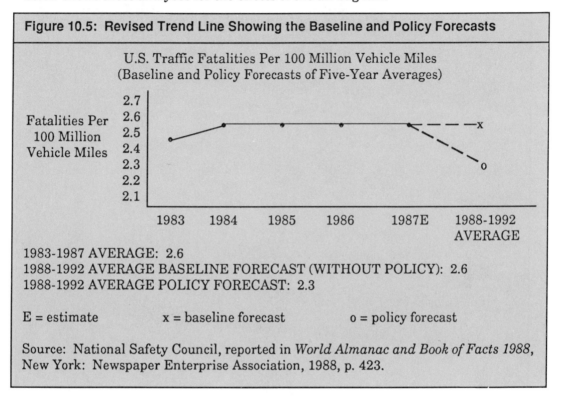

Figure 10.5: Revised Trend Line Showing the Baseline and Policy Forecasts

U.S. Traffic Fatalities Per 100 Million Vehicle Miles
(Baseline and Policy Forecasts of Five-Year Averages)

1983-1987 AVERAGE: 2.6
1988-1992 AVERAGE BASELINE FORECAST (WITHOUT POLICY): 2.6
1988-1992 AVERAGE POLICY FORECAST: 2.3

E = estimate   x = baseline forecast   o = policy forecast

Source: National Safety Council, reported in *World Almanac and Book of Facts 1988*, New York: Newspaper Enterprise Association, 1988, p. 423.

On the following pages are the worksheets containing the example Exercise 10.3 demonstrating the effects of the Teen Court on drug-related arrests of teens.

EXAMPLE

EXERCISE 10.3: MAKING A POLICY FORECAST

(A) DESCRIBE THE EXPECTED CHANGES IN THE IMPACT AND TREND ESTIMATES FOR EACH OF THE FIVE FACTORS AS A RESULT OF IMPLEMENTATION OF THE PROPOSED POLICY: Proposed Policy: Establish a Teen Court

FACTOR	BASELINE FORECAST ESTIMATES IMPACT	TREND	NEW ESTIMATES (IF DIFFERENT) IMPACT	TREND	REASONS FOR DIFFERENCES
1. Police crackdown	-1	0	same	same	
2. No. of teen-agers	+2	0	same	same	
3. No. of sentences	-3	-2	same	0	Teen courts will at least stop the decline in the number of sentences.
4. Drug availability	+3	+3	same	same	
5. Education programs	-1	+1	same	+2	The publicity about the teen courts will be an additional way to spread the message against drug abuse.

(B) INSERT THE NEW ESTIMATES AND CALCULATE THE FIVE-YEAR POLICY FORECAST:

FACTOR	IMPACT (-3 TO +3)	TREND (-3 TO +3)	CALCULATION 1 IMPACT SCORES
1. Police crackdown	-1	0	(1)
2. No. of teens	+2	0	(2)
3. No. of sentences	-3	0	(3)
4. Drug availability	+3	+3	+9
5. Education programs	-1	+2	-2

CALCULATION 2: Sum of positive scores plus 1/2 of scores in parentheses = 12
CALCULATION 3: Sum of scores ignoring signs and parentheses = 17.00
CALCULATION 4: Calculation 2 divided by Calculation 3 = .71
CALCULATION 5: Calculation 4 + .5 = 1.21
CALCULATION 6: Calculation 5   x   Historical average = 5-year policy forecast
                    1.21   x   17.40 = 21.1

(continued)

168

EXERCISE 10.3 (continued)

(C) REPRODUCE THE TREND LINE GENERATED FOR STEP 10.1 AND ADD THE BASELINE AND POLICY FORECASTS FOR FIVE-YEAR AVERAGES. USE AN "x" TO INDICATE THE BASELINE FORECAST, AND AN "o" TO INDICATE THE POLICY FORECAST:

TITLE:The Effect of Teen Courts on the Forecast of Drug-Related Arrests
Reported by the Police, Riverdale
March 1988

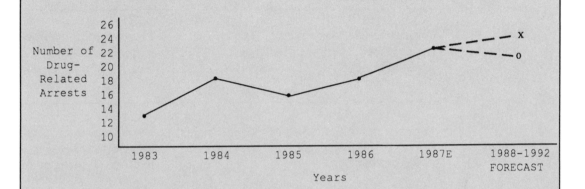

1983-1987 AVERAGE: 17.4
1988-1992 AVERAGE BASELINE FORECAST (WITHOUT POLICY): 24
1988-1992 AVERAGE FORECAST ASSUMING POLICY IS IMPLEMENTED: 21

E = estimate   x = baseline forecast   o = policy forecast

Source: 1983-1986, Riverdale Police Records, reported in the February 1987 issue of the <u>Riverdale Times</u>, p. 1

169

SUMMARY

CONCEPTS	DEFINITIONS	TASKS	EXAMPLES
Variable	Numbers measuring a cost or benefit of a policy	Clearly define how the cost or benefit will be measured	The percent of civilian population actively looking for work who cannot find work from 1982 to 1987.
Baseline Forecast	Forecast made assuming the proposed policy is not implemented	Use Impact System	Forecast of unemployment rate assuming no passage of a jobs program
Policy Forecast	Forecast made assuming the proposed policy is implemented	Revise Impact System	Forecast of unemployment rate assuming passage of a jobs program
Impact or Factor	The extent to which the factor influences a variable to increase or decrease	Estimate a number between +3 and -3	Peer approval of drug use has a +3 impact on drug use
Trend of Factor	Whether the factor will increase, decrease, or stay the same in the future	Estimate a number between +3 and -3	Peer approval of drug use will show -2 trend in the future

PART V: IMPLEMENTING A PUBLIC POLICY

In Part V, you will work through a model for forecasting the probability that a policy will be implemented. You will also explore the development of political strategies for affecting that probability. Finally, you will re-evaluate your policy using your newly acquired policy analysis skills.

Chapter 11: Forecasting Implementation with the Prince System

Step 1: Describing the Policy to Be Implemented

Step 2: Identifying the Players

Step 3: Estimating Issue Position, Power, and Priority for Each Player

Step 4: Completing the Prince Chart and Calculating the Probability of the Policy Being Accepted

Chapter 12: Developing Political Strategies

Step 1: Selecting a Player for Developing a Strategy

Step 2: Constructing a Prince Political Map

Step 3: Describing a Political Strategy

Step 4: Assessing the Impact of the Strategy

Chapter 13: Revising Policy Analysis

CHAPTER 11

FORECASTING IMPLEMENTATION WITH THE PRINCE SYSTEM

YOUR GOAL

To forecast the chances that a policy will be implemented.

INTRODUCTION

Good public policy ideas do not become policies without sufficient political support. A method for forecasting the chances that a policy will be implemented is the **Prince System**.

The Prince System, named after Machiavelli's famous book, *The Prince*, is a technique for assessing the relative support and opposition of various individuals, groups, and organizations for a public policy decision. The Prince System requires that you do the following:

1. Identify the **players** likely to have a direct or indirect impact on the decision.

2. Determine **issue position**–whether each player supports, opposes, or is neutral toward the decision.

3. Determine **power**–how effective each player is in blocking the decision, helping make it happen, or affecting the implementation of a decision.

4. Determine **priority**–how important the decision is to each player.

5. Calculate the likelihood that the policy will be implemented.

You will learn how to perform each of these steps in this chapter.

172

STEP 11.1
DESCRIBING THE POLICY TO BE IMPLEMENTED

Begin by clearly describing the public policy you wish to see implemented. Using your preferred alternative developed in Exercise 8.5, obtain information on the following:

1. Level of government at which the policy will be implemented–local, state, federal, or international.

2. Legislative requirements–does the policy require a new or revised law?

3. Administrative and financial requirements–what agency will be primarily responsible and what funds, if any, are required?

4. Judicial decisions–how will court interpretation affect the policy?

Be sure that you have defined a policy and not a goal. For example, "reducing unemployment" is not a policy but a goal. "Spending $100 million of federal funds to provide job-training programs" is a policy.

Although the policy needs to be clearly described in order to forecast its implementation, the exact details of its final formulation are not required. Frequently, policies are altered to gain the support needed for their implementation. For example, the 1986 tax reform bill started out with tax rates lower than those that eventually appeared in its final version. The Prince System can be applied to a proposed policy and then applied a second time to a revised policy.

EXAMPLE

EXERCISE 11.1: DESCRIBING THE POLICY
TO BE IMPLEMENTED

(A) BRIEFLY DESCRIBE THE POLICY YOU WANT TO IMPLEMENT. INCLUDE THE UNIT OF GOVERNMENT INVOLVED:

The Riverdale Youth Bureau should create a court with teenagers as judges to try and sentence youths eighteen and under accused of buying, selling, and using drugs. The Teen Court would sentence the offenders to rehabilitation, community service, and time serving on the Teen Court. This program will be controlled by the County Youth Bureau.

(B) INDICATE THE LEGISLATIVE REQUIREMENTS FOR THE PROPOSED POLICY:

New legislation is not needed for implementation of the policy, and all administrative duties will be performed by the program director.

(C) INDICATE THE ADMINISTRATIVE AND FINANCIAL REQUIREMENTS FOR THE PROPOSED POLICY:

The court will be administered by a new staff person whose salary, expenses, and administrative costs will total $36,000.

(D) INDICATE THE JUDICIAL REQUIREMENTS FOR THE PROPOSED POLICY:

No formal court action is required, but the District Attorney and the Town Justice would have to agree to allow this court to operate informally.

STEP 11.2
IDENTIFYING THE PLAYERS

Reasons for including a player are any of the following:

- The player has substantial legal authority.
- The player has political influence to promote or obstruct the decision. (Players that can prevent the policy from being implemented are *veto players*.)
- The player has formal or informal influence on a veto player.

Identifying the players to be considered is one of the most important steps in the Prince System. Omitting an important player can distort the analysis so much that it becomes useless.

A key to identifying the correct players is to consider the legislative, financial-administrative, and judicial requirements of the policy. If the proposed policy involves monetary decisions, include players that have authority over the budget. If the proposed policy requires revised or new legislation, include the chief executive and the legislature. If the policy requires neither new funds nor new legislation, include the bureaucracies responsible for the policy and those that influence those bureaucracies. In addition to government officials in the executive and legislative branch, include players representing key interest groups.

To develop your list of players, begin by writing down all those you think are relevant. Next, reduce the list to between five and ten of those on your list that are essential.

The principal way to limit the number of players is to group individuals and organizations into collective players for the purpose of analysis. The process of grouping frequently appears arbitrary and can seriously affect the results if it is not done carefully. Guidelines that assist in grouping players to improve the accuracy of the analysis include the following:

- Group players having the same economic interests. In dealing with an environmental issue, for example, all private developers might be grouped together.

- Do not group players with veto power. This especially holds for governmental players. For example, in federal legislation, never group the President and Congress.

175

- Do not group players if there is a disagreement among them or if their components have widely unequal power. For example, members of a city government could be combined as a single player if there were general agreement among them concerning the issue and if each person in the governing unit had approximately equal power. If there were disagreements, or if some members were much more powerful than others, it would be preferable to divide them into two (or more) players.

- Select a list of players that represents a reasonable picture of the overall power distribution. Do not include an excess of players that gives one side unrealistic weight. If there is one collective player with an immense amount of power, that player should be divided into enough smaller players so that the total power is accurately reflected. For example, in dealing with the executive branch, you might want to list the President and the Cabinet as separate players rather than treat the executive branch as a single player.

These guidelines are intentionally quite general. Your judgment in conducting the analysis is vital at every step. Rely on the Prince System as a way of organizing and guiding your analysis. Your success depends on your becoming knowledgeable enough to select the right group of players.

EXAMPLE

EXERCISE 11.2: IDENTIFYING THE PLAYERS

LIST AT LEAST FIVE PLAYERS AND INDICATE WHY THEY HAVE BEEN INCLUDED IN YOUR LIST. THE TOTAL SET OF PLAYERS SHOULD FAIRLY REPRESENT THE RANGE OF SUPPORT AND OPPOSITION TO THE PROPOSAL:

1. PLAYER: James French, District Attorney of Riverdale

   REASON: His consent, with that of the judge, is necessary to create the court.

2. PLAYER: Joyce Zeno, County Youth Bureau

   REASON: She is responsible for approving youth related programs in the county.

3. PLAYER: K. Westcott, Deputy Director for Local Services in Division for Youth

   REASON: She has the authority to allocate funds for youth programs in the state.

4. PLAYER: J. McGrath, Chief of Riverdale Police

   REASON: The Chief would have to cooperate with the District Attorney and the Town Justice for the program to operate effectively.

5. PLAYER: Johanna Horton, Town Justice

   REASON: Her consent, along with that of the District Attorney, is necessary to create the court.

177

STEP 11.3
ESTIMATING ISSUE POSITION, POWER, AND PRIORITY FOR EACH PLAYER

Issue Position is the current attitude of the player toward the policy. It is expressed as a number ranging from +5 to -5 to indicate levels of support or opposition. A +5 is assigned if the player is firmly in favor of the issue and is unlikely to change; a +4, +3, +2, or +1 indicate lower levels of firmness of the player's support. A neutral position is expressed as 0. Similarly, a -5 indicates firm opposition, while a -4, -3, -2, or -1 indicate lower degrees of opposition. When estimating a player's issue position:

- Read and listen to what the player says about the issue.

- Estimate from the player's economic, social, or political standing what the player's position is likely to be on the basis of self-interest.

- Look for differences among individuals and factions within groups and organizations. Look for inconsistencies in statements by individual members. If the contrasting positions seem evenly balanced, assign a 0 (neutral) issue position. If there seems a slight positive or negative balance toward the issue, assign a +1 or -1 for the player's issue position.

Power is defined as the degree to which the player, relative to the other players, can directly or indirectly exert influence concerning the decision on policy implementation. The basis of a player's power is based on such factors as group size, wealth, physical resources, institutional authority, prestige, and political skill. Power is expressed as a number ranging from 1 to 5. A 1 is assigned if the player has a slight amount of power; a 2 if the player has more than minimum power; a 3 or 4 if the player has substantial power; a 5 if the player can veto or prevent the implementation of the policy with little or no interference by other players. When estimating a player's power:

- Ask if the player has the ability either to block or implement the policy.

- Determine if legal authority is a consideration and if the player possesses a large share of the authority.

- Consider whether a player has the ability to help or hinder the carrying out of a decision.

- Determine, if need be, how much wealth the player has.

- Do not assume that a player, powerful on one set of issues, is necessarily powerful on all issues.

- Consider the allies and enemies of the player. Powerful allies increase power, while powerful enemies diminish it.

178

Priority is defined as the importance that the player attaches to supporting or opposing the decision relative to all other decisions with which that player is concerned. Priority is expressed as a number ranging from 1 to 5. A 1 indicates slight interest or concern for the issue regardless of the player's issue position and power. A 2 is assigned for those players with some concern, while a 3 and 4 indicate substantial concern. A 5 is reserved for those players that assign the highest priority to the issue.

When estimating priority:

- Determine the frequency and intensity with which the player makes public statements about the issue.

- From the player's social, political, and economic interest, determine the importance the player is likely to attach to the decision.

- Watch out for the fact that priority can be rapidly and substantially altered by external events and the intrusion of other issues.

- Remember that other issues and factors compete for the player's attention and, hence, priority.

As with selecting players, the assignment of issue position, power, and priority requires good information and a solid understanding of the financial-administrative, legislative and judicial factors affecting the policies. Systematic research can play an important role, but the importance of the skillful assessment of existing conditions by knowledgeable and sensible observers is absolutely essential. Therefore, you have to be thoroughly familiar with the situation to provide accurate estimates on issue position, power, and priority. You should talk to other knowledgeable people and gather all available information on the reactions of individuals, groups, and organizations to the proposed policy. Refer to Chapters 4 and 6 for information-gathering skills.

EXAMPLE

EXERCISE 11.3: ESTIMATING ISSUE POSITION, POWER, AND PRIORITY FOR EACH PLAYER

ESTIMATE AND PROVIDE JUSTIFICATION FOR THE ISSUE POSITION, POWER AND PRIORITY FOR EACH PLAYER LISTED IN EXERCISE 11.2:

NAME OF PLAYER ONE: James French

ISSUE   +1   James French feels that the Teen Court is worth a try but fears that high school students may not be morally developed enough to make these decisions about other teens.

POWER: 5   His power is high because, as District Attorney, his consent, with that of the judge, is necessary to create the court.

PRIORITY: 1   His concern is with prosecuting all people who break the law, without partiality to any particular offenders.

NAME OF PLAYER TWO: Joyce Zeno

ISSUE :   +4   Joyce Zeno believes the Teen Court would be a refreshing new way to attack the drug problem.

POWER: 5   She has a lot of power because she is director of the bureau that would implement the program.

PRIORITY: 3   She gives the issue high priority. She recently wrote a letter to the editor of the newspaper expressing the need for community concern on the issue.

NAME OF PLAYER THREE: K. Westcott

ISSUE :   -2   K. Westcott opposes the proposal because she favors the traditional court system with stiffer penalties.

POWER: 5   Her power is high because she allocates the funds for youth programs in New York State.

PRIORITY: 1   Her priority is low because the Teen Court is only one of the many youth programs in the state with which she deals.

(continued)

180

EXAMPLE

EXERCISE 11.3 (continued)

NAME OF PLAYER FOUR: J. McGrath

ISSUE: -4   J. McGrath opposes the program because he feels teens will see this as just a way to avoid a jail sentence.

POWER: 3   As police chief, McGrath has authority and influence in local government and the community and can indirectly affect the implementation of the Teen Court.

PRIORITY: 3   He is concerned about the drug issue but has many other criminal issues with which to deal on his job.

NAME OF PLAYER FIVE: Johanna Horton

ISSUE: 0   Johanna Horton's issue position is neutral because she thinks that the penalties might not be stiff enough, but she does acknowledge that teen courts have been successful in other communities.

POWER: 5   The implementation of the program depends on her cooperation as she has final jurisdiction over the offenders.

PRIORITY: 3   She gives some priority to the drug issue, but also is concerned with other lawbreakers.

STEP 11.4
COMPLETING THE PRINCE CHART AND CALCULATING THE PROBABILITY OF THE POLICY BEING ACCEPTED

After the estimates of issue position, power, and priority are made for each player, you can determine the probability that the policy will be implemented. The steps for estimating this probability are illustrated in the following example, based on a proposed policy for a university to raise its tuition.

Figure 11.1: Prince Chart

POLICY: Raise Tuition in the Next Academic Year
(STATE IN TERMS OF DESIRED POLITICAL OUTCOME.)

Calculation 1

PLAYERS	ISSUE POSITION -5 to +5	X	POWER 1 to 5	X	PRIORITY 1 to 5	=	PLAYER'S PRINCE SCORE
Administration	+2	X	3	X	3	=	+18
Board of Trustees	0	X	2	X	2	=	(4)
Student Government	-3	X	1	X	2	=	-6
Faculty Senate	+2	X	3	X	2	=	+12
Parents Office	-2	X	2	X	1	=	-4
Budget Committee	+2	X	1	X	3	=	+6

CALCULATION OF PROBABILITY:

Calculation 2:   *Sum of all positive scores plus 1/2 neutral scores = 38*
Calculation 3:   *Sum of all scores ignoring signs and parentheses = 50*
Calculation 4:   *Probability of support = Calculation 2 ÷ Calculation 3*
$$= \frac{38}{50} = .76 \ (76\%)$$

Calculation 1: Issue Position x Power x Priority = Prince Score

Multiply issue position, power, and priority for each player to determine the player's Prince Score. For example, the Administration in Figure 11.1 has an issue position of +2, a power of 3, and a priority of 3. The product of these three numbers is +18. If the issue position is 0, multiply just the power and priority to determine the player's Prince Score, and put a parenthesis around the score. For example, the Board of Trustees has a 0 issue position, a power of 2, and priority of 2, leading to a Prince Score of (4).

Calculation 2: Sum of All Positive Scores Plus 1/2 Neutral Scores

Find the sum of all positive Prince Scores plus 1/2 the sum of all Prince Scores that are enclosed in parentheses (the neutral scores). In this case, the sum of all positive Prince Scores is 36 (Administration is +18, Faculty Senate is +12 and the Budget Committee is +6). The neutral score is 4 for the Board of Trustees. Add 1/2 of 4, or 2, to the 36 for a total of 38 for this calculation. If the neutral score is an odd number, round up.

Calculation 3: Sum of All Scores Ignoring Signs and Parentheses

Find the sum of all Prince Scores ignoring signs and parentheses. In this case, the sum of all scores is 50. (Administration is 18, Board of Trustees is 4, Student Government is 6, Faculty Senate is 12, Parents Office is 4, and the Budget Committee is 6.)

Calculation 4: Probability of Support = Calculation 2 ÷ Calculation 3

Divide the number you found in Calculation 2 by the number you found in Calculation 3. In this case, it would be 38 divided by 50 which equals .76 or 76%. The calculation of the probability for the policy analyzed in the Prince Chart in Figure 11.1 indicates that there is 76% chance that tuition rates will increase. In other words, this forecast indicates that the chances are quite high that the rates will increase.

Interpretation of Probability	
100%	— Certain to be implemented. (In case of 100% agreement on a policy, then by definition, there would be no public policy issue.)
60% – 99%	— Likely to be implemented.
40% – 59%	— Uncertain. Likely to continue being disputed without resolution.
1% – 39%	— Unlikely to be implemented. Most likely to be killed as a proposal.
0%	— Never will be implemented. (In case of 0% support of a proposal, there is no public policy issue.)

EXAMPLE

EXERCISE 11.4: COMPLETING THE PRINCE CHART AND CALCULATING THE PROBABILITY OF THE POLICY BEING ACCEPTED

(A) USING THE POLICY AND PLAYERS DEVELOPED FOR EXERCISES 11.2 AND 11.3, PLACE ESTIMATES OF THE ISSUE POSITION, POWER, AND PRIORITY FOR EACH PLAYER IN THE PRINCE CHART BELOW. THEN CALCULATE THE PLAYERS' PRINCE SCORES:

POLICY: _____Establish a Teen Court_____
(STATE IN TERMS OF A DESIRED POLITICAL OUTCOME.)

Calculation 1

PLAYERS	ISSUE POSITION	X	POWER	X	PRIORITY	=	PLAYER'S PRINCE SCORE
James French	+1	X	5	X	1	=	+5
Joyce Zeno	+4	X	5	X	3	=	+60
K. Westcott	-2	X	5	X	1	=	-10
J. McGrath	-4	X	3	X	3	=	-36
Johanna Horton	0	X	5	X	3	=	(15)

(B) CALCULATE THE PROBABILITY:

Calculation 2: Sum of all positive scores plus 1/2 neutral scores = 72.5
Calculation 3: Sum or all scores ignoring signs and parentheses= 126
Calculation 4: Probability of support=Calculation 2 divided by Calculation 3

$$= \frac{72.5}{126} = .575 = (58\%)$$

(C) WRITE A BRIEF INTERPRETATION OF THE RESULTS OF YOUR CALCULATIONS:

There is a 58% chance the policy will be implemented. Since the chance is close to 50% and it is uncertain whether the policy will be implemented, the policy will continue to be disputed.

184

SUMMARY

CONCEPTS	DEFINITIONS	EXAMPLES
Issue Position	Support, opposition, or neutrality that a player has on a proposed policy	The President has an issue position of +5 on his tax reform bill
Power	Ability of player to influence the implementation of a policy	Because the President can veto a tax bill, he has a power of 5
Priority	Degree to which the player considers the proposed policy important	The President considers tax reform more important than any other legislation
Prince Chart	Display of relevant players with their issue position, power, and priority	See Figure 11.1

PARTICIPATION ACTIVITY: Providing Political Forecasting to Players

1. Select a policy issue that you (or your group) would be interested in studying.

2. Identify a specific player that is interested in the selected issue. Contact the player directly by phone or mail. If you have trouble contacting the actual player or one of the player's assistants, you can still undertake the project and submit it without prior contact. However, it is better to get help from the player at the outset. If you are unable to arrange a meeting, skip the next step and go directly to 4.

3. Explain to the player that you would like to prepare a study assessing the chances that a proposed policy will be implemented or an existing policy be altered. Ask for suggestions on how to clearly describe the policy and how to get information on the relevant players, including their issue position, power, and priority.

4. Produce a report that describes the positions of each player and your estimate on the chances of the policy being implemented (if it is proposed) or remaining in effect (if it is in existence but controversial). Conduct a Prince Political Analysis following the guidelines described in this chapter. You may not want to include the actual Prince Chart in your report because the player may not be familiar with the technique. However, the Prince Political Map might be included and described to help the player understand your analysis.

5. Complete the report on the agreed-upon date, submit it in written form, and offer to make an oral presentation.

6. Thank the player for the opportunity to provide the service. Provide a report to the class on your experience.

CHAPTER 12

DEVELOPING POLITICAL STRATEGIES

YOUR GOAL

To develop strategies for affecting the chances that the policy will be implemented.

INTRODUCTION

In Chapter 11, you learned how to forecast the likelihood that a proposed policy would be implemented. That analysis is based on the information you have about political support and opposition at a given time. However, political support and opposition can change constantly as a result of elections, new social conditions, or even accidents. For example, the support for large government expenditures on drug education increased substantially in 1986 when well-known athletes died from drug overdoses.

Among the main sources of change are the actions different players take to support or oppose a policy. For example, Mothers Against Drunk Driving (MADD) threatened to oppose legislators seeking re-election if they did not vote for strong DWI laws. These actions are called strategies because they are taken to achieve a specific goal—to increase or decrease the likelihood that a policy will be implemented.

In this chapter, you will learn how to formulate a strategy using the information you developed in Chapter 11.

187

STEP 12.1
SELECTING A PLAYER FOR
DEVELOPING A STRATEGY

The first step in developing a strategy is to determine whether or not you want a policy implemented. You can make a decision on the basis of your own feelings about the policy or select a position based on other considerations. The exercises in this chapter require you to develop a strategy on behalf of one of the players in your Prince analysis from Chapter 11.

Select a player that has a firm issue position and high priority. Don't select a player unless it has a score of at least 3 on both factors. The reason for this is that players with scores of less than a 3 on issue position and priority are not likely to pursue a strategy since they themselves are open to changing their position and do not care enough to take strong action.

Your selection of a player may also depend upon your knowledge of the player's power. Select a player with a significant amount of power because more strategies are likely to apply.

EXAMPLE

EXERCISE 12.1: SELECTING A PLAYER FOR DEVELOPING A STRATEGY

FROM YOUR PRINCE ANALYSIS IN CHAPTER 11, SELECT A PLAYER WHICH HAS AN ISSUE POSITION OF 3 OR MORE AND A PRIORITY OF 3 OR MORE. PROVIDE A JUSTIFICATION FOR YOUR CHOICE:

NAME OF PLAYER: Ms. Joyce Zeno

REASON FOR SELECTION:

Ms. Zeno has a lot of power (5) in her position as Director of the Youth Bureau. Thus, she can utilize a wide variety of strategies. Her issue position is a +4 which means she has a firm position in support of the policy. She also gives the Teen Court policy a moderate priority (3), so she will work hard to change the positions of others.

STEP 12.2
CONSTRUCTING A PRINCE POLITICAL MAP

As an aid in developing a strategy based on the information provided in the Prince Chart, construct a Prince Political Map. It is a display of the information you have in the Prince Chart, so that you can see where you would like players to be in order to achieve your goal. Location on the vertical axis is determined by the player's issue position. Location on the horizontal axis is determined by multiplying the player's power times priority. An example of a Prince Political Map appears in Figure 12.1 below. It is based on the sample Prince Chart of the decision to raise tuition that was discussed in Chapter 11.

Figure 12.1: Prince Political Map of Raising Tuition

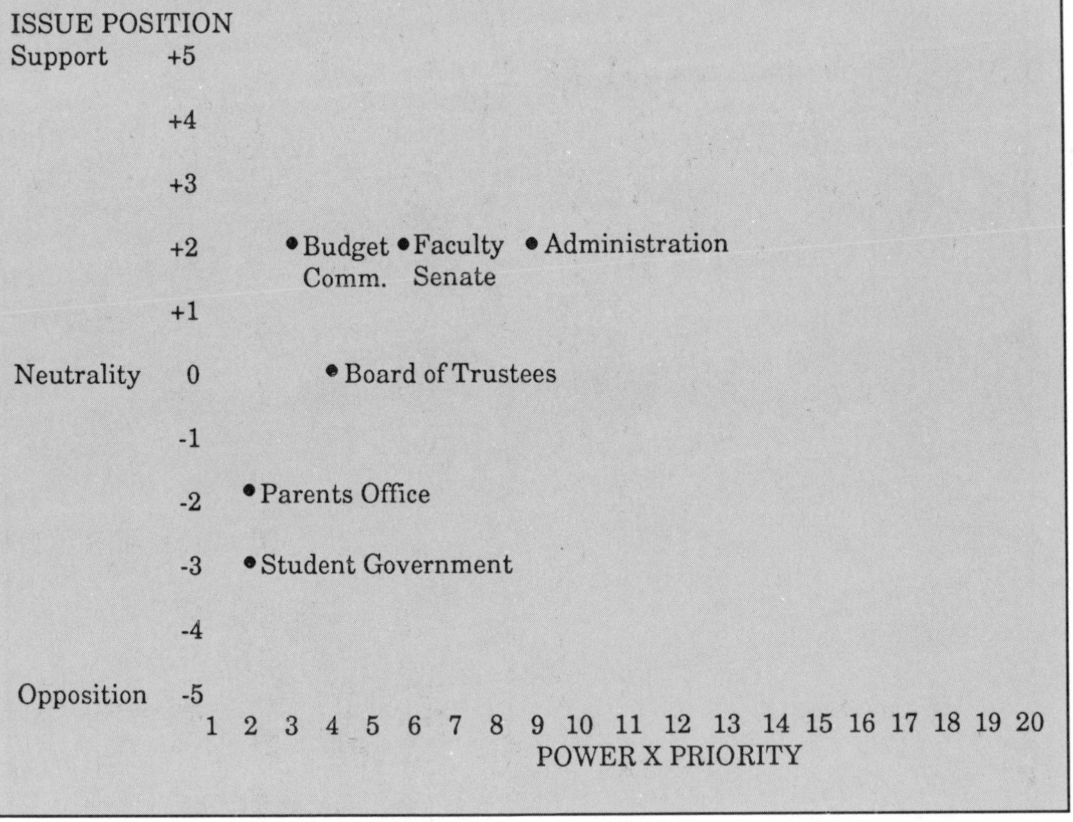

ISSUE POSITION

Support   +5

           +4

           +3

           +2   ● Budget ● Faculty   ● Administration
                     Comm.   Senate

           +1

Neutrality 0   ● Board of Trustees

           -1

           -2   ● Parents Office

           -3   ● Student Government

           -4

Opposition -5
              1 2 3 4 5 6 7 8 9 10 11 12 13 14 15 16 17 18 19 20
                                    POWER X PRIORITY

190

EXAMPLE

EXERCISE 12.2: CONSTRUCTING A PRINCE POLITICAL MAP

USING THE INFORMATION CONTAINED IN EXERCISE 11.3, IDENTIFY THE POLICY AND PLACE THE PLAYERS IN THE APPROPRIATE PLACES ON THE PRINCE MAP BELOW:

PRINCE POLITICAL MAP OF _____ Establishing a Teen Court _____

ISSUE POSITION

Support   +5

          +4   • Joyce Zeno

          +3

          +2

          +1   • James French

Neutrality   0   • Johanna Horton

          -1

          -2   • K. Westcott

          -3

          -4   • J. McGrath

Opposition -5

              1 2 3 4   5 6 7 8 9 10 11 12 13 14 15 16 17 18 19 20 21 22 23 24 25

POWER X PRIORITY

191

STEP 12.3
DESCRIBING A POLITICAL STRATEGY

You are now ready to select specific actions to increase the support for your player's position on the issue. Your goal is to take actions that move players on the Prince Map so the situation becomes more favorable to you:

- If your goal is to increase the chances that the policy will be implemented, move as many players as possible toward the upper right-hand corner of the map.

- If your goal is to reduce the chances that the policy will be implemented, move as many players as possible toward the lower right-hand corner of the map.

- For players that have a firm position opposite to yours, move them as far toward the left-hand side of the map as possible.

Your strategy need not cause a complete shift; any movement in the directions indicated above is an improvement.

To move players around on the Prince Political Map, four basic strategy goals are available:

- Add new players that will occupy the position you want on the map or delete players that now occupy positions on the map that are undesirable from your point of view.

- Change the issue position of players.

- Change the power of players.

- Change the priority of players.

In planning your strategic action, it is important to distinguish between strategy goals and the strategies to achieve these goals. Strategy goals include various desired changes that would alter probability as you wish it to be altered. Strategies are the specific actions you decide to take to achieve your goals. For example, a goal might be to raise players' priorities. The strategy to achieve that goal might be to issue a statement to the news media that will raise the players' priority levels.

Strategies for Achieving Strategy Goals*

1. *Add new players or delete existing players.*

This strategy goal can radically alter the chances of a decision, but it is very difficult to implement. For any public policy issue, players in the game are not likely to leave. The exceptions are politicians who lose elections and individuals with health or personal problems. New players might be added as a result of elections, and campaigning actively for certain candidates would be a strategy to achieve that strategy goal. Adding new players can also be accomplished by creating new organizations. For example, various students who support a particular school policy change could establish a formal organization as a strategy.

2. *Change the issue position of players.*

This strategy goal is the most frequently sought. Its effectiveness depends on the power and skill of the player using it and the attitudes of the target players. There are four basic ways to change a player's issue position:

- Make specific promises to do something in exchange for a shift in issue position. In legislatures, this is called logrolling, when one legislator supports one bill in order to win another legislator's support on another issue. Campaign contributors promise money in exchange for support promised by candidates.

- Redefine the policy to accommodate the interests of those opposed without sacrificing the essential ingredients of what you want. This is usually called compromise and is found in all kinds of political bodies that make decisions.

- Make threats to do something unpleasant if the player does not shift position. Lobbyists and legislators sometimes resort to threats if promises do not work.

- Make arguments that use facts and emotional appeals to change the player's mind. This strategy is always necessary, but it cannot be used by itself. It must be accompanied by other strategies in order to work.

*A computer program that enables you to evaluate the effect of Prince Strategies is "The Prince Political Forecasting System," Policy Studies Associates, 1987.

The four ways to change issue positions of players are listed in the order of general effectiveness. Promises and compromise are less costly than threats to the player pursuing the strategy. Arguments are made by all players all of the time. Although arguments are a necessary ingredient to any strategy, they never work by themselves. Threats are costly because they can backfire. The player might stick to its own position even more firmly. Threats, therefore, should be used only as a last resort.

The firmer a player's issue position, the more difficult it is to move that player. If the player is on your side, a firm position indicates a reliable ally. If the player is on the opposite side, firmness is a measure of how difficult it will be to get your strategy to work. If you move a player that is -5 to a +1, the chances of success are increased more than if you move a -1 player to a +1. However, it is easier to move the -1 player to a +1. You often have to choose between a sure chance of a small gain against a small chance of a big gain.

3. *Change the power of yourself and other players.*

Power comes from a variety of sources, including:

- Appointed or elected position in the policy-making process

- Wealth

- Organizational size and cohesion

- Reputation for knowledge

- Number and importance of friends and enemies

Increasing the power of your allies and decreasing the power of your opponents take a long time and a great deal of work. However, there may be no other choice. Remember, you obtain maximum results from power strategies if you direct them at players with firm positions and high priority.

194

4. *Change the priority of other players.*

Priority strategies fall into three categories:

- Trying to raise priority by creating events that generate publicity or distributing information on the issue.

- Trying to lower priority by keeping the issue quiet or generating other issues that take your issue out of the spotlight.

- Trying to raise or lower priority by compromising or redefining a proposed policy.

Use publicity with care. It is not always to your advantage to raise the priority of all players. If your opponents have high priority and those who support you have lower priority, raising priority will improve your situation. However, if your supporters already have high priority and your opponents don't, raising priority will hurt you. In fact, in this last instance, your strategy goal should be to lower priority among players.

To formulate an effective political strategy, once you have decided on the player you wish to represent, examine the Prince Political Map and do the following:

- Decide on which players you wish to concentrate.

- Consider the four types of strategy goals just presented.

- Select a strategy that will move players in the direction you want.

Make sure that the player you represent can actually carry out the strategy. Spell out the specific steps that might be taken to execute your strategy.

EXAMPLE

EXERCISE 12.3: DESCRIBING A POLITICAL STRATEGY

DISCUSS A STRATEGY THAT MIGHT BE PURSUED BY THE PLAYER SELECTED IN EXERCISE 12.1 TO STRENGTHEN THE OUTCOME THE PLAYER FAVORS. STATE WHAT SPECIFIC ACTION(S) THE PLAYER WILL TAKE:

Joyce Zeno will try to decrease opposition to the policy by using the strategy of compromise. She recognizes James French's concern that teens may not be morally developed enough to make such mature decisions. She will propose creating an advisory board to review the decisions made by the court. This board would consist of herself, Mr. French, and members of the community who are interested and knowledgeable about the issue.

STEP 12.4
ASSESSING THE IMPACT OF
THE PROPOSED STRATEGY

Once you have described your strategy, discuss its impact. Forecast how each of the players on the Prince Political Map will be affected by the strategies. Examine the effects of your strategy on each player even if the strategy is designed to work primarily on only one. Remember that the players are constantly keeping track of one another; there will be some indirect effects of any strategy you pursue.

To assess the impact of your strategy:

1. Provide a brief comment on what changes you expect with respect to issue position, power, and priority as a result of your strategy.

2. Draw arrows on the Prince Political Map prepared in your original analysis showing how players will move as a result of your strategy.

3. Recalculate a new Prince Chart with the changed issue position, power, and priority scores.

Remember also that different strategies have different effects on different players. Promises, compromises, threats, and arguments will change only the issue position of players. Increasing publicity through such actions as petitions, pickets, and demonstrations will raise priority, but may not change either issue position or power. Most power strategies take a long time to be effective and may affect several players. For each player, whether a direct target or not, consider what the impact of the strategy will be.

EXAMPLE

EXERCISE 12.4: ASSESSING THE IMPACT OF THE PROPOSED STRATEGY

(A) BRIEFLY DESCRIBE THE IMPACT OF THE STRATEGY YOU DEVELOPED IN EXERCISE 12.3. FOR EACH PLAYER LIST THE ORIGINAL ISSUE POSITION, POWER AND PRIORITY SCORES. LIST THE NEW SCORES PRODUCED BY YOUR STRATEGY. IF THE SCORES REMAIN THE SAME WRITE AN "S." PROVIDE A REASON FOR THE CHANGES:

PLAYER	ORIGINAL SCORE	NEW SCORE	REASONS
James French	Position +1 Power 5 Priority 1	+3 S S	His main reservation was the possibility that teens might not make responsible decisions. If there is an adult board to oversee the decisions, he is willing to give the policy more of a chance.
K. Westcott	Position -2 Power 5 Priority 1	S S S	The compromise does not change her opposition. She still favors the traditional court system.
J. McGrath	Position -4 Power 3 Priority 3	-2 S S	He was afraid the teens would just see the Teen Court as a way to avoid a jail sentence. His opposition to the proposal is less as he thinks an adult advisory board may be able to monitor this. He does not support the proposal because he still has reservations.
Johanna Horton	Position 0 Power 5 Priority 3	+1 S 2	She feels that the board could monitor the penalties and make sure they are stiff enough. Thus, she gives slight support to the policy. Her priority declines because she is no longer concerned that there will be negative effects from the policy.

(continued)

198

EXAMPLE

EXERCISE 12.4 (continued)

(B) DRAW ARROWS ON THE PRINCE POLITICAL MAP COMPLETED IN EXERCISE 12.2.*
COMPLETE THE PRINCE CHART BELOW SHOWING THE CHANGES RESULTING
FROM YOUR STRATEGY. CALCULATE THE NEW PROBABILITY:

Calculation 1

PLAYERS	ISSUE POSITION -5 to +5	X	POWER 1 to 5	X	PRIORITY 1 to 5	=	PLAYER'S PRINCE SCORE
James French	+3	X	5	X	1	=	+15
Joyce Zeno	+4	X	5	X	3	=	+60
K. Westcott	-2	X	5	X	1	=	-10
J. McGrath	-2	X	3	X	3	=	-18
Johanna Horton	+1	X	5	X	2	=	+10

CALCULATION OF PROBABILITY:

Calculation 2: Sum of all positive scores plus 1/2 neutral scores = 85

Calculation 3: Sum of all scores ignoring signs and parentheses = 113

Calculation 4: Probability = Calculation 2 divided by Calculation 3

$$= \frac{85}{113} = .75 \quad x \quad 100 \quad = \quad 75\%$$

* The next page shows an example of the map in Example Exercise 12.2 with the arrows
drawn. You should draw arrows on the map you produced in Exercise 12.2.

199

BELOW IS A REVISED EXERCISE 12.2 , A PRINCE POLITICAL MAP WITH ARROWS FORECASTING THE EFFECT OF THE PROPOSED STRATEGIES.

PRINCE POLITICAL MAP OF___ Establishing a Teen Court

ISSUE POSITION

Support   +5

            +4   • Joyce Zeno

            +3

            +2   • Johanna Horton (arrow)

            +1   • James French

Neutrality   0

            -1

            -2   • K. Westcott

            -3

            -4   • J. McGrath

Opposition -5
            1 2 3 4 5 6 7 8 9 10 11 12 13 14 15 16 17 18 19 20 21 22 23 24 25

                          POWER X PRIORITY

SUMMARY

CONCEPTS	DEFINITIONS	EXAMPLES
Strategy Goals	Desired changes in issue position, power, and priority of players	Raise priority of all players
Strategies	Plan for changing the issue position, power, and priority of the players	The President promises to help Congressmen who supported him on tax reform in their reelection campaigns
Prince Political Map	A display of the location of players with respect to issue position and power times priority	See example in Figure 12.1

PARTICIPATION ACTIVITY: Providing A Political Strategy To Players

1. Select a policy issue that you (or your group) would be interested in studying.

2. Identify a specific player that is interested in the selected issue. Contact the player directly by phone or mail. If you have trouble contacting the actual player or one of the player's assistants, you can still undertake the project and submit it without prior contact. However, it is better to get help from the player at the outset. If you are unable to arrange a meeting, skip the next step and go directly to 4.

3. Explain to the player that you would like to prepare a report suggesting what strategies might be pursued to help implement a favored policy. Ask the player to review your analysis of the chances the policy will be implemented and make adjustments based on the player's comments. Ask the player for ideas about possible strategies and what has been tried in the past.

4. Produce a report that begins with a presentation of the Prince Map and that discusses the current chances of the policy being implemented. Describe possible strategies the player could undertake using the guidelines in this chapter. For each strategy, discuss the impact using arrows on the Prince Political Map. Indicate a ranking of the strategies from most effective to least effective and suggest how much each would increase the chances of the policy being implemented. If possible, offer to assist the player in implementing the strategy (assuming you support the player's goal).

5. Complete the report on the agreed-upon date, submit it in written form, and offer to make an oral presentation.

6. Thank the player for the opportunity to provide the service. Provide a report to the class on your experience.

CHAPTER 13

REVISING POLICY ANALYSIS

YOUR GOAL

To apply policy analysis skills to a selected policy.

INTRODUCTION

The purpose of this chapter is to apply what you have learned since you made your policy alternative selection in Step 8.5 and to reach a conclusion concerning your initial policy selection.

In the five previous chapters, you went through a series of steps that began with identifying a social problem, proposing a public policy to deal with that problem, forecasting the impact of that policy and analyzing the chances of the policy being implemented. The critical stage in the analysis was the selection of the policy alternative which is Step 8.5.

In selecting the policy in Step 8.5, you were asked to weigh the benefits and costs as well as the political feasibility of your proposed policy against the benefit and costs as well as political feasibility of alternative policies. Because you had not conducted the analysis required in Chapters 9, 10, 11 and 12 prior to Step 8.5, your initial judgment was not as informed as it now would be.

As a result of your additional knowledge and analysis, you should now reach one of the following conclusions:

1. Your policy as stated was the best among the alternatives you suggested.

2. Your policy was on the right track, but it needs revision because of uncertainty about its benefits and costs (covered in Chapters 9 and 10) or because of questions about its political feasibility (covered in Chapters 11 and 12).

3. One of the other policy alternatives considered in Chapter 8 would be better than the one you have been analyzing.

4. A completely new alternative would be preferable.

As a final activity, review the work you have completed in Chapters 8 – 12. Write a brief essay describing one of the four conclusions above, and justify your conclusion. Use the analysis techniques of Chapter 10, Chapter 11, and Chapter 12 to justify your conclusion. Use the analysis techniques as follows:

1. If you decide your policy is better than any alternatives, use Chapters 9, 10, and 11 to analyze the most viable alternative and show why your choice is preferable.

2. If you choose options 2, 3, or 4 above, repeat the analyses in Chapters 9, 10, 11, and 12 to indicate the advantages of your new proposed policy.

Use the following outline to justify your final choice:

I. Executive summary. In no more than one page describe the stand you have taken, summarizing the main points of your proposed policy.

II. Summarize the social problem with which your policy is intended to deal.

III. Formulate your policy using the procedures in Chapter 8. Compare your policy with the most comparable current policy dealing with the same problem.

IV. Summarize the benefits and costs of your policy. Provide a baseline forecast and policy forecast helping to show the relative benefits of the policy.

V. Summarize the political feasibility of the policy. Recommend a set of strategies to overcome political opposition to the policy.

Appendix A: The New York Times As An Information Source

This appendix introduces *The New York Times* as a source of information in the study of public policy issues. One of the world's leading newspapers, it provides an excellent source of current information on public policy issues affecting the United States and the New York metropolitan area. It also provides some coverage of public policy issues affecting other states and local areas within the United States and many countries. What makes *The New York Times* the newspaper of choice for introductory public policy analysis is the substantial background material and level of detail provided in its regular coverage and the fact that most political leaders view it as a source of information that will affect the evolution of public policy .

Exercises that require the use of newspaper articles should be completed using recent issues of *The New York Times*. Those exercises are 1.1 and 1.2; 3.1–3.6; and 7.2–7.7.

In addition, the in-depth study of public policy issues required for Chapters 8 through 12 should begin with a study of past and recent articles of the newspaper. Back issues of the paper are available on microfilm as indicated in Exercise 4.7.

Overall Content and Organization

If you become familiar with its content and organization, you can use *The New York Times* as a powerful tool for the study of contemporary public policy issues. Here is how the editors of the newspaper suggest that you use *The New York Times* every day.

You don't read a newspaper the way you read a novel or a textbook or even a magazine. A paper like *The New York Times* is carefully organized so you can read it quickly. Headlines are written so you can get basic information even when time is very short.

A great many *Times* readers give themselves a quick overview of the paper as soon as they get it in the morning. It's simple to do, and it gives you a very good idea of what's going on. The investment in time: 15 minutes or less!

First, they read all the headlines on page 1. Just the headlines alone give them a good idea of the major events of the day (the subheads give them even more information). Most people do this in less than a minute.

Next, they turn to the first page of the second section. It's called Section B, Metropolitan News. Here is where readers find major stories about events and developments throughout the tri-state area, consisting of New York, New Jersey and Connecticut. For a quick idea of what's happening in the business world, they flip to the first page of Section D, *Business Day*, for the Business Digest which gives them an idea of what they'll be able to read later in that section. By following their example, for an investment of less than five minutes on this step, you will already know more than you could have found out anywhere else in twice the time.

The next step, which takes less than 10 minutes, is to go through the paper page-by-page, reading the headlines, looking at pictures, skimming an occasional article. People who do this don't usually have the time to read for details, but they learn a lot about what's going on in the world before they start their day, and they're far ahead of the game when they do.

If you follow a system like this for yourself, you'll probably come up with variations of your own to suit your own time schedule and range of interests. A newspaper like *The New York Times* becomes a very personal thing. It stays with you all day and it's there when you need it, ready to tell you about things you want to know. Any time you want to know them.

In general, *The Times* is organized in the same fashion every day. Understanding how it's organized helps you find your way to your special interests in less time.

It all begins with page 1, of course. It's where the editors put the "best" stories. What's meant by "best" could be the most important. It could also be the most unusual or most readable. The emphasis a newspaper places on any of these qualities determines the character of that newspaper.

The New York Times puts its first emphasis on the important. But it doesn't neglect the other qualities at all. In fact, you'll probably find all of them represented on a typical Times front page: articles that are not only important news, but also about unusual items and special interest stories. But since *The Times* believes its first duty is to inform, not just entertain, things you should know about always take precedence.

You'll be able to know what the editors considered the most important story of the day because it will be placed to the top of the last column on the right. This may seem odd because we read from left to right. But the custom is related to two other customs. First, newspapers used to be arranged on newsstands folded with just the upper-right-hand corner showing. Second, *The Times* used to be arranged so that the lead story on page 1 continued from the bottom of that page to the top of page 2. Both of those old customs have changed, but the basic arrangement of *The Times'* front page has not.

The size of the headline over the top of the lead story is another clue to its importance. Occasionally, but not often, the headline extends across the top of the whole page. When it does, it's called a "banner headline."

The day's second-most important story appears at the top of the column at the extreme left. An exception to that rule is when the two most important stories are related to each other. Stories in similar fields are usually grouped together to help you find your way and to keep your own thinking organized.

Most page 1 stories "jump" or are continued on pages inside the paper. Here, too, the same kind of organization applies. A business news story would be continued in the Business Day Section. A story from Washington would be finished in the first part of the paper, Section A.

Related stories always appear together, and the news is arranged in general classifications. Foreign news appears on the first few pages of the first news section. It's followed in the same section by the national news report. Local news from New York,

206

New Jersey and Connecticut, follows in the Metropolitan News, Section B. And business news is found in Section D, Business Day.

You may find something related to public policy in *Science Times* which is a special section appearing each Tuesday. A feature story on a space probe or an adventure to the bottom of the sea. A story on a breakthrough in medicine or a new clue to man's ancestors from the middle of a desert. It can be a look at the past, a glimpse of the future.

Education is part of *Science Times*, too, and a special column, *Education*, usually begins on the first page. Inside, you'll sometimes find reviews of new books on science or a column on medicine, *The Doctor's World*. You'll find answers to readers' questions about science there, and a column called *Science Watch* with brief reports on new scientific trends. You'll get more education news inside *Science Times*, along with a special weekly column, *About Education*.

Types of Articles on Public Policy Issues

Three types of articles can be found on public policy issues:

1. ***News stories***—reports of events that constitute the social conditions, the government actions, or activities of players concerning a specific public policy issue. (These terms are described in Chapter 1 of this book.) They include such stories as:
   "Study Warns of Inadequate Housing," *New York Times*, March 15, 1988, p.B4.
   "New Jersey Transit Seeks to Raise Fares 9%," *New York Times*, February 24, 1988, p.B1.
   "Large Infusion of Funds Urged for Public Works," *New York Times*, February 25, 1988, p.A11.

2. ***Background analysis***—articles that provide historical perspectives or specific information about social conditions, players, or government actions. Sometimes these may accompany a specific news story. At other times, background analysis may be presented as a result of studies carried out by reporters or analysts. They include such stories as:
   "Overcrowding Pervades Prison Life in Connecticut," *New York Times*, March 21, 1988, p.B2.
   "U.S. Family Income Is Up, But Not Uniformly," *New York Times*, February 27, 1988, p.B1.
   "Smoke Clears and Trains Are Cleaner," *New York Times*, March 1, 1988, p.B1.

3. **Opinion pieces**—editorials prepared by the editorial board of the newspaper, letters to the editor, or brief essays prepared by people who have a particular point of view. These articles appear on the two pages prior to the last page of Section A. They are called "opinion pieces" because when they cover public policy topics they express the views of the writer on the benefits or costs of existing policies and social conditions or on what government or non-government institutions should do about social conditions. Typical examples of opinion pieces are:

>Howse, Jennifer L. "New York City's Shameful Infant-Mortality Rate," *New York Times*, March 17, 1988, p.A26.
>Smpadian, Susan "Dissolve the Taxi Commission and Start Again," *New York Times*, January 26, 1988, p.A24.
>"The Promise of Liberty Scholarships," *New York Times*, January 27, 1988, p.A26.

These three types of articles frequently do not appear in pure form. Any given article may have elements of all three types. News stories will often have extensive background information and may report the opinions of players or experts on what policy should be followed. Background analysis can be found in the editorial pages and is frequently stimulated by news events. Opinion pieces sometimes start with the description of a recent news event and are designed sometimes more to provide background rather than express opinion on what should be done. However, for any given article, it is relatively easy to classify the article as primarily a news story, a background or an opinion piece.

Where to Find Information on Public Issues

You will need to be able to locate news articles, background analysis, and opinion pieces relevant to public policy issues to complete many of the exercises in this book and to build an information base for public policy issues you wish to study indepth. Of course, the editors and reporters of *The New York Times* do not announce at the beginning of an article that it is about a specific public policy issue. Rather they write about such things as new laws, which politicians are supporting what proposals, statistics on specific social conditions such as crime rate, unemployment and reading scores of high school students. They also report specific events such as meetings of government officials, judicial decisions or public statements.

It takes a little imagination to determine whether a given article is related to a public policy issue. Here are a list of some that fit the bill. Note that several do not specifically mention a public policy issue but are close enough to warrant inclusion.

The newspaper itself is organized in a consistent way so that you can expect to find certain types of public policy issues discussed in certain sections. The table on the following page gives some general guidelines.

208

Table: Types Of Public Policy Issues

Types	Section of the Paper
International—includes American foreign policy and major events and conditions in other countries.	First part of Section A
US national	After first four pages in Section A and possibly beginning on first page if important
New York metropolitan area includes city, suburbs, New Jersey, and Connecticut suburbs.	Section B unless major news event, then on A.
Business and economic	Section D unless major event then begins on A
Sports issues involving government policy	Sports Sections daily and Section C on Mondays
Science and technology questions as well as research background on any issue; also education issues	Section C, Science Times published every Tuesday

Articles from *The New York Times* should be used in completing Exercises in Chapters 1, 3, and 7. For Chapters 8 through 12, you are expected to use additional sources as well, to become as knowledgeable as possible on your public policy issue. In order to do that, you will need to check on a systematic basis for stories relevant to your topic. Although you may choose a topic that is not covered directly in *The New York Times* because it is a local community issue or a state issue not of significant importance to the tri-state area, you should still perform a quick search on every issue of the newspaper in case information on related topics are included. The skimming process indicated on pages 205–206 of this Appendix is recommended.

In addition, you should take advantage of the index available on page B1. It is an index and news summary and will tell you if there is a major story related to your topic.

You should also know about *The New York Times Index* which will allow you to examine through microfilm any article published in *The Times* on your topic. Step 4.7 provides you with information on how to use the *Index*.

Appendix B:
Student Guide to Participation in the Good Society Exercise

OVERVIEW

You are about to participate in a two-period exercise in which you will be a member of one of eight groups—Central Authority and Groups A through G. Your group is defined in two ways—by the number of its Goods and by the number of its Power Weights. "Goods" refer to the wealth each group enjoys; "Power Weights" refer to the group's influence in making decisions about the distribution of both Goods and Power Weights. Your goal is to achieve what you think is best for your group and for the society as a whole. The Good Society is based on the principles of justice, order, freedom, and equality.

Distribution of Wealth and Power Weights

Name of Group	Goods	Power Weights
Central Authority	100	3
Group A	45	2
Group B	35	2
Group C	10	1
Group D	8	1
Group E	4	1
Group F	4	1
Group G	4	1
TOTAL	210	TOTAL 12

PROCEDURE

The exercise is divided into two class periods. During the *first* period, you will meet in a group to which you have been assigned. You will choose a representative, decide on a goal for your group, plan a strategy to achieve that goal, and provide a public statement for the *Good Society News*. During the first period, *one* representative from each of the groups (A-G) and *three* representatives from Central Authority will be allowed to visit the members in the other groups to discuss plans. The meeting time will run about fifteen minutes and will take place in the middle of the period.

During the *second* period, a representative for each group will meet under the direction of a representative from Central Authority in front of the members of all of the groups. A discussion will be held on the various views about the existing distribution of Goods and Power Weights in the Good Society. This discussion will last for about 15 minutes, after which there will be a 15 minute period for representatives to meet with their groups and other groups. After that period, the discussion will continue in the front of the room.

During either the first or second day, any group or Central Authority may circulate a petition calling for the restructuring of either Goods or Power Weights. A successful Petition must have the signatures of enough members of the society so that at least seven Power Weights are represented on the Petition. A signature is valid only if all members of the groups or Central Authority agree to the Petition. When a Petition is signed and submitted to the Instructor and after the Instructor verifies that it is a valid Petition, the new distribution indicated in the Petition goes into effect. Additional Petitions can be developed and signed, but they must be based on the Power Weight distribution in the previous Petition that has been legally implemented. Goods can only be redistributed and must always sum to 210. Power Weights can be redistributed, decreased, or increased.

Two forms are required for the exercise. The first is a Statement Form on which each group and Central Authority indicates its goal, its strategy, its representative, and the statement it wants to release publicly. The other form is the Petition Form on which changes in the distribution of Goods and Power Weights can be indicated.

GOOD SOCIETY PETITION FORM

Description of Change

	New Goods Distribution	New Power Weight Distribution
Central Authority	___	___
Group A	___	___
Group B	___	___
Group C	___	___
Group D	___	___
Group E	___	___
Group F	___	___
Group G	___	___
TOTAL	210*	TOTAL ___

Which Groups Have Signed

	Power Weight	Signatures
Central Authority	3	_____
Group A	2	_____
Group B	2	_____
Group C	1	_____
Group D	1	_____
Group E	1	_____
Group F	1	_____
Group G	1	_____

*Goods cannot be added or deleted. The total for Power Weights can be changed.

GOOD SOCIETY STATEMENT FORM

Group Name_____

Representative_____

Goal (Be specific about the preferred distribution of Goods and Power Weights)

_____

_____

_____

_____

Strategy

_____

_____

_____

Public Statement to Appear in *The Good Society News*:

GLOSSARY OF TERMS
as used in *Public Policy Skills*

abstract – a type of index which provides brief summaries of articles

administrative acts – an action taken by government to put a law into practice

almanac – a resource providing both statistical and general descriptive information

arc – any section of the line that outlines a circle or a curve

attitudinal information – information that indicates how people feel and what they think about social conditions or about public policies designed to deal with those conditions

bar graph – method of displaying data using parallel bars allowing comparison of quantitative information for different years, locations or other units

baseline forecast – forecast made assuming the proposed policy is not implemented

benefit – a desirable consequence of a public policy

blue pages – a section of the phone book that lists all government offices (federal, state, county, local) in the area

citation – the proper format used when documenting the use of a book

closed-choice response – a type of question in which the respondent has a limited number of alternative answers

cluster sampling – a method in which the subjects to be interviewed are chosen in clusters or groups

cost – undesirable consequence of a public policy

Dewey Decimal System – a system by which books are arranged and categorized

dictionaries – books which primarily give short definitions, proper spelling, pronunciation, syllabification, and information on the origin of words

encyclopedias – general or specialized books that define both terms and concepts, giving broader definitions than dictionaries

equality – the idea that each member of a community is equal to other members of the community

evaluating social conditions – applying goals to determine whether social conditions are desirable or undesirable

event – 1) an action in a specific time and place by an identifiable person, group, or institution; 2) a physical occurrence at a particular time and place

evidence of a problem – information that documents the existence of undesirable social conditions

explaining social conditions – providing reasons for past and present conditions

factor – a circumstance or condition that contributes to a problem

factual information – actual information that can be measured

forecasting social conditions – projecting conditions into the future

214

general index – an index covering a large number of periodicals on a variety of subjects

goal – preferred social condition motivating players

graph – a diagram used to display data

impact of factor – the extent to which the factor influences a variable to increase or decrease

indexes – a reference to locate articles published on a specific period of time. Information within an index is arranged alphabetically by subject, author, and title

individual freedom – the right of the individual to think, speak, and act as they wish as long as it does not infringe on the freedom of others

international – the level of government at which policies involve two or more national governments or international organizations

issue position – support, opposition, or neutrality that a player has on a proposed policy

journal – a publication containing articles designed for scholars, analysts, and players in the policy-making process

judicial decisions – the application of the law to a specific situation

justice – the fair treatment of individuals by the government, others in society, and before the law

knowledgeable people – people who have specialized information on a public policy issue

legislation – behavioral guidelines established to be followed by members of society

level of public policy – level at which government action takes place. Levels most often used are local, state, national, and international

Library of Congress System – system by which books are arranged and categorized

local – level of government in which policies apply to either a village, town, city, or county

magazine – a publication containing articles and advertising; has many readers

means – policy pursued to achieve a goal

microform – any form of photographically reduced documents or print; the most frequently used are microfilm and microfiche

monitoring social conditions – observing and recording what is happening in society that gives rise to a public policy issue

national – the level of government in which policies apply to the entire United States

national security – the ability of a country to defend itself against the domination or physical destruction by a foreign army

non-random sampling – a procedure in which subjects are not selected by chance

open-ended response – a type of question in which the respondents can answer in their own words

Pearson's r – a correlation statistic, appropriate to interval and ratio scale data

percentages – a precise indication of the difference between two (or more) periods of time, locations, or other types of units

215

pie chart – a display to show how a quantity is divided into parts

players – individuals, organized groups, or institutions that consciously work to shape public policy

policy forecast – forecast made assuming the proposed policy is implemented

power – the ability of a player to influence the implementation of a policy

prescribing public policy – suggesting a government action to create a preferred social condition

Prince Chart – a display of relevant players with their issue positions, power, and priorities

Prince Political Map – a display of the location of players with respect to issue position and power times priority

priority – the degree to which a player considers the proposed policy to be important

private interest – a goal pursued for the direct benefit of the player

problem – an undesirable social condition

public interest – a goal assumed to benefit the whole society

public policy – the actual or proposed government action intended to deal with the social condition

public policy issue – an issue involving a public policy, its impact on social conditions, and conflicting players

quantitative data – information giving or being measured in specific numbers

random sampling – a sampling procedure in which all subjects have an equal chance of being selected

sample – a group of subjects whose responses would be representative of the population as a whole

sampling bias – the factors in the sampling procedure which may cause the information to be inaccurate

scatterplot – (or scatter diagram) a graph that shows types of association of variables

simple random sampling – a method in which each subject is chosen from a complete list of members of the target population through a process in which each unselected subject has the same chance of being selected as any other subject on each draw

social conditions – the economic and social indicators including the physical environment, and people's behavior and attitudes, that can be traced to the public policy in question

social order – the maintenance of peace and the consistent operation of laws within a society

state – the level of government in which policies apply to one of the 50 states in the United States

statistical source – a book where specific statistical information concerning a wide range of topics can be found

strategies – plans for changing the issue position, power, and priority of the players

strategy goal – desired change in issue position, power, and priority of players

subject index – index covering a large number of periodicals on one general topic

subject index – index covering a large number of periodicals on one general topic

subject title index – an index covering only one publication or title

survey – a way of gathering information about social conditions and people's attitudes

survey of events – a resource providing information on recent happenings

table – a method of displaying data that allows comparison of quantitative information for different years, locations, or other units

target population – the group of people to which the survey applies

trend of factor – whether the factor will increase, decrease, or stay the same in the future

trend line – a graph showing past, present, and future projection of data for a period of time

variable – numbers measuring a cost or benefit of a policy

yearbook – a resource providing both statistical and general descriptive infor-